MOVING TO MEXICO

THE EASY WAY

A No-Nonsense Guide to NORTHERN BAJA for Expats, Digital Nomads, and Retirees

CHERI SICARD

For Mitch Mandell, my brother from another mother,
who first went on this Baja adventure with me,
changed his life for the better, and never looked back.

Moving to Mexico the Easy Way:
A No-Nonsense Guide to Northern Baja
for Expats, Digital Nomads, and Retirees

Contents

Introduction:
The Joys of Northern Baja
California, Mexico

Have you ever considered living outside the United States, but the expense and logistics seem too daunting?

I'm going to let you in on the secret of the absolute quickest, easiest, and least expensive way to move outside of the U.S. This place will slash your living expenses by 30-50% or more while still allowing you to maintain the convenience of U.S. services like mail, health care, vehicle registrations, and more. I call it "expat light living," and you can find it just over the border in the northern part of Mexican state of Baja California.

Less expensive than the U.S., northern Baja is breathtakingly beautiful, you'll find a plethora of diverse things to see and do, the food is amazing, and so are the warm people and laid-back lifestyle. But for some reason, most of the expat publications and relocation guides ignore this area, which is why I decided to write this book.

Maybe it's because Baja does not have the famous big, flashy tourist attractions of Mexico City, Tulum, Puerto Vallarta, San Miguel de Allende, et al. Or even of Los Cabos on the southern end of the Baja peninsula, which is over a thousand miles from the border. But what it lacks in these, it more than makes up for in natural beauty and convenience. Not to mention, sometimes fewer tourists is a good thing, although Baja has no shortage of tourists.

While it might not be as well-known as other parts of Mexico, the northern region of Baja offers plenty, including 1000s of miles of gorgeous beaches, Mexico's premier wine region, unparalleled fishing, surfing, and water sports of all kinds, great golfing, world-class off-roading, cosmopolitan cities, and remote off-grid eco-tourism destinations. And despite what you may have heard, it's safe, a topic I cover in detail in chapter 3.

Semantics: Baja, Baja Norte, Baja Sur, The Baja

This book focuses exclusively on relocating to the northern part of Baja California, Mexico, or *Baja Norte*. No, "norte" is not officially in this Mexican state's name, as it is in *Baja California Sur* (south), located on the southern part of the Baja peninsula. However, I will occasionally use the terms *norte* or north in this book to clarify what area we are referring to. Just know that the official state name is *Baja California*, not *Baja California Norte*.

One more picky semantic point that brings out the trolls in social media groups: you will sometimes hear certain Americans refer to the region as "The Baja," thinking this makes them sound "in the know." In fact, it does just the opposite. I have been going to Baja, and now living there, for well over five decades, and I have never ever heard a Baja resident refer to it as "the Baja" (your results may vary according to the trolls). In my experience, the lowdown is this: In the same way that New Orleans residents will never call their city "Nawlins," every time I have ever heard someone refer to "The Baja" it was a dead giveaway that the person talking was a tourist who didn't know all that much about the place they were talking about.

My Baja Story

I had been visiting Baja my whole life long before I made the move to the small village of Punta Banda, just south of Ensenada, in 2017 (don't Google it, it will bring up a VERY different place - Google *La Bufado*ra or *Ejido Esteban Cantu* instead and you will see the general area).

At the time and like so many others, my best friend and I were endlessly struggling to afford US housing, food, insurance, and fuel costs. We paid a fortune to live in Los Angeles and had nothing left over at the end of the month with which to enjoy the benefits of the amazing city we called home.

We had been casually considering Mexico for a while when a short but memorable road trip with friends over Thanksgiving to visit Ensenada and the Valle de Guadalupe wine country convinced us to take the plunge. And we've never regretted it.

We found a warm, welcoming, accepting community of both locals and expats. In fact, I affectionately call Punta Banda my "Mexican Mayberry." There are communities like it all over northern Baja.

Both of us applied for and received our permanent resident cards. Even better, my friend found love, got married, and is now living happily ever after in a beach house steps from the sand.

When I first moved to the Ensenada area, I honestly thought it would be a stopping point in a journey much further south. But I found the convenience of having the best of both worlds, Mexico and the United States, a strong draw. I still had family in Southern California I could visit at any time. I could keep the healthcare providers I knew and liked. It was easy to keep a U.S. mailing address, and many more conveniences that would be far more logistically challenging and/or expensive if I lived farther away. Plus, Ensenada is a fabulous city and the surrounding area offers so much to see and do.

This book explains how we made the move and what was involved. I wrote it to address the most common questions and concerns about moving to Northern Baja and to provide a road map for those who want to try it out themselves.

The places I discuss are all less than three hours from the US border, many of them far closer than that. And don't worry—it's not all hearts and flowers. I understand that living in Mexico is not for everyone, and I will do my best to point out the downsides too. In fact, I devote an entire chapter to it. However, in my experience, the upsides far outnumber the downsides.

Without a doubt, the Northern part of Baja is the easiest way for Americans to dip their toes into the experience of living in another country without having to uproot EVERYTHING and relocate to another part of the planet. After all, if you don't like it, you can always just drive back over the border to the States and restart your old life.

But you probably won't...

Cheri Sicard

February, 2025

PART 1
Considering Baja

In this section of the book, I'll cover the common concerns people have about moving to Baja. In the meantime, here are some advantages of relocating to Baja to ponder:

18 reasons to consider moving to Baja California

- Its proximity to the US gives you the best of both worlds.
- You can save 30-50% or more in living expenses over US prices.
- Keep your U.S. car registration if you want.
- Keep a U.S. address if you want.
- Keep your U.S. bank accounts if you want.
- Keep your U.S. medical care if you want.
- While it's a good idea to learn the language, English is prevalent enough to easily get by without speaking Spanish.
- Mexico has relatively easy immigration rules.
- You'll find warm, welcoming communities of natives and expats.
- Affordable beachfront living!
- The wine country and the foodie culture that comes with it.

- Incredible seafood (and fishing).
- World-class off-road racing.
- World-class water sports including surfing, snorkeling, diving, kayaking, sailing, and more.
- Cosmopolitan cities, rural villages, or remote off-grid natural living choices.
- A varied geography of oceans, deserts, and mountains.
- Large American (and Canadian) expat communities and resources.
- The tacos. (No, I am not kidding, the tacos are out of this world and cheap!)

Chapter 1: Why Move to Baja Norte?

Economics will be a driving factor for most people moving to Baja. Are there cheaper places in the world to live? Certainly. There are even cheaper places in Mexico to live. Baja is known for having higher-priced goods and services than many other Mexican states. That said, for the most part, they are still about 30 to 50% less than in the U.S., depending on where you are coming from. If you live frugally in Baja, your savings can be substantially higher than that.

Location, location, location! This is another driving force that makes Baja an excellent expat choice for so many people. Proximity to the United States, especially the metropolis of San Diego and all its services and infrastructure, offers a strong draw. There is outstanding shopping there where you can buy any of the foods or brands you might be missing from home. You'll also find a large international airport there.

But there's more to being so close to San Diego. For instance, many west coast Baja residents commute for healthcare at the excellent medical facilities and hospitals, including a large VA hospital for veterans.

Some people even commute to work in the San Diego area while enjoying the lower-priced living of Tijuana or Rosarito. I have even met a few people who commute for work from Ensenada, but this is a far longer drive (2 hours plus) and most had friends or relatives on the U.S. side that they could stay with during the work week.

On the eastern side of the peninsula, it's a quick hop over the border to Calexico, California.

Auditioning Baja Living

The proximity to the U.S. makes it reasonably easy to take Baja life out for a test drive before fully committing to moving there. I highly recommend doing so because, as we will discuss in Chapter 4, moving to Mexico is not for everyone.

If you have the time, I recommend finding a short-term rental in an area where you think you might want to move. Spend a few weeks or even months there. Try to give yourself time to explore and check out other neighborhoods or even cities, too, as you may find something you like better.

I'll talk more about this in Chapter 8, but another advantage to getting a short-term rental first is that you will often encounter places and deals on housing when you are there that you could never have found online.

Gringo and Expat: They Are NOT Slurs!

A lot of foreigners hold the mistaken belief that being called a *gringo*, and you WILL be called a *gringo* in Mexico, is somehow a slur or an insult. Don't make this mistake. Being referred to as a *gringo* does not mean any disrespect, it simply means you are a foreigner as opposed to a native. However, if it has a rude Spanish epithet in front of the word *gringo* that's another matter. So being called a *gringo* is OK, a *pinche gringo*, not so much. Learn how to avoid this in Chapter 12.

Throughout this book, I use the term expat. Some people who don't understand what the word means bristle at this term. However, according to the Oxford Dictionary, expat simply means a person who lives outside their native country. It does not denote anything else. You need not give up your love of, or patriotism to, your native country when you are an expat.

How to Get Around When Exploring Baja

Having a car is the easiest way to explore various areas in Baja, especially for those living in Southern California and Arizona. Just buy insurance (see sidebar), and drive around and check out your options.

The main toll road highway that runs down the coast from Tijuana to Ensenada and beyond is a beautiful, well-maintained road, as is the road to San Felipe from Mexicali.

However, know that once off these main thoroughfares, Baja's roads are notoriously ill-maintained. Stay vigilant, as you can encounter rough patches, axle-busting potholes, speed bumps, dirt roads, and even livestock on the pavement. Find more information on driving in Baja in Chapter 3.

Bringing Foreign Vehicles to Baja

Vehicles are another reason moving to Baja is simpler than other locales, even other locales in Mexico. That's because Baja has special rules regarding foreign vehicles, and those rules work in your favor.

If you plan to drive in most of Mexico, a Temporary Vehicle Permit (TIP) is required. However, the good news is that the entire Baja peninsula, north and south, is exempt from this requirement, as are any "border zones," meaning areas within 25 kilometers (16 miles) of the border. That's one less piece of legal paperwork to worry about. But wait, it gets even better.

In most of Mexico, legal permanent residents MUST register their vehicles with Mexican license plates. This can be a bureaucratic hassle, to the point that many people hire a service to help them accomplish it. However, because of Baja's special rules, U.S. license plates and registrations can be used there without restrictions, even when you are a permanent resident.

It seemed too good to be true, so I double-checked with my Mexican attorney, Carlos Victorica Reyes, and he confirmed it. However, he clarified that this rule only covers you in the Mexican states of Baja,

Baja Sur, and the border zones. If you want to drive in mainland Mexico and you don't want to change your U.S. registration, you will have to sign a voucher stating the vehicle will not remain there for longer than six months and limit your time to that.

Many northern Baja expats never let go of their U.S. registrations and plates. Some keep registrations in their home states or wherever they keep their U.S. address, often California. Others save money by registering vehicles in South Dakota, a state long friendly to out-of-state nomads such as RVers and expats. South Dakota offers lower registration rates and lax laws regarding how much time "residents" are required to spend in the state. However, know that South Dakota's laws concerning out-of-state vehicle registrations are a politically-charged hot topic in the state and likewise under constant debate, and possibly changing. Check the current status before transferring your vehicle registrations.

Bringing Your RV to Baja

If you have an RV, that can provide a great way to explore northern Baja, or it can provide a cost-efficient temporary residence while you use your smaller vehicle to explore. You will find RV parks on both coasts, as well as in the Valle de Guadalupe (more on these locations in Chapter 2).

I have traveled back and forth over the San Ysidro border many times, first in a small Class B motorhome, and later towing a 25-foot travel trailer without incident.

If you have a large rig you can get to Ensenada and points north on the Pacific coast, or to San Felipe on the Gulf Coast, without much trouble. The toll roads are well-maintained. However, I do not recommend cruising around Baja in large rigs. The roads in remote areas are narrower, lack shoulders, are not always in great condition, and are prone to unexpected livestock on the pavement. This leads to stressful driving that will beat up your rig unless your RV is made for off-roading. Do people take bigger rigs south in Baja? Sure. But as a lifelong RVer with lots of experience, I would not personally advise it.

That said, remote Baja is an amazing van lifer or truck camper's off-grid playground!

One more note: RVs are more apt to be searched both when coming into Mexico as well as when leaving the country to go back to the U.S. I have been searched every time I have entered Mexico in an RV. That said, I have never had an extensive search where they tore through everything. I have been lucky to this point and crossing the border in my RV has never been much of a hassle. But others have reported longer waits involving more thorough searches. Surprisingly, I have not been searched every time going back into the U.S. with an RV. Most of the time, but not every time.

IMPORTANT: Mexican Auto Insurance

You are required to have a supplemental Mexican insurance policy on your vehicle and/or RV when driving in Baja. You can purchase a policy online, or there are places at the border on the U.S. side where you can buy insurance.

I have always used *Baja Bound* as they have had the best prices, and their service has a good reputation. So far, I have not had any accidents and have not had to put it to the test (and hope I never will). I can say the customer experience of getting insurance through them is super easy. Their website also has lots of terrific travel information, and they also insure U.S. rental cars if your rental agency authorizes Mexico travel.

Baja Bound Mexican Insurance - bajabound.com

Other Ways to Get to Baja

Those who are not close enough to drive over the border have four options, listed in order of expense, least to most:

#1 Public Transportation: When coming from the States most Americans will likely find it easiest and most affordable to fly into San Diego, CA. Catch the Blue Line trolley at the San Diego airport and take it to the end of the line at the San Ysidro border (see san.org). Walk across the border to the Tijuana bus terminal and catch a comfortable ABC bus to go wherever you want to go in Baja. For more information, see abc.com.mx.

The modern luxury ABC buses are a terrific option for traveling between cities and regions in Baja.

Once in Baja cities, and even some outlying areas, you'll find lots of micro-buses (privately owned public transportation vehicles). Micro-buses are what the locals who don't own cars use. They can help you get around town and are extremely inexpensive, although some knowledge of Spanish will help you navigate them.

You can also use taxis and Ubers in some larger cities to get around.

#2 Rent a car: Do not just rent a car in the US and drive it over the border into Mexico as you will be in violation of your rental agreement. That said, most major US car companies have some allowances for driving into Mexico, but they all come with caveats and restrictions. Check with your preferred car rental company about renting a car to go into Mexico. Most of them will have this fine print:

- You must have a corporate account.
- You must purchase Mexican insurance (which you must do with your own car too).
- You cannot drive more than 250 miles south of the border.

Other restrictions may apply.

Alternately and less restrictively, you can walk across the border and rent a car in Tijuana. Find rental agencies at the bus terminal within walking distance (or a quick cab ride) from the border.

#3 Hire a driver: If you want to hire a driver to chauffeur you around Baja, it's both doable and affordable. To set things up before you go, I suggest making inquiries in the Facebook group(s) of the area or even the community where you want to go. Learn more about the importance of using Facebook groups for expats in Chapter 12.

If you are already in Baja, know that the larger cities like Tijuana and Ensenada have robust cab service infrastructures. They also have Uber. Even though it is against Uber's official rules, most Uber drivers are more than happy to contract with you independently, so if you find a driver you like, it never hurts to make friends, inquire, and make a deal.

#4 Work with a realtor and/or relocation service: Those same Facebook groups that will help you find a driver can also help you find a realtor or a relocation service. If you have the funds to hire one, a good relocation service can help you find the right area of Baja to suit your needs and temperament, they can help you find your dream house, condo, or apartment to buy or rent, they will take you on tours of various areas, and they can also help streamline the entire move to your new life.

I don't have personal experience with many of these services, but I have definitely encountered a number of Baja realtors that I would steer clear of. Always research and trust your intuition when evaluating any service provider in Mexico, regardless of whether the provider is a native or an expat.

One service I can recommend is GV Baja Realty in the Ensenada area. No, I am not getting paid to say it, but Gabriela Victorica McEntee has consistently demonstrated the height of professionalism, and I have never heard a bad word about her or her work. If that's not enough, her dad is immigration attorney Carlos Victorica Reyes, who can help with attaining temporary or permanent residence in Baja (He did my permanent residence paperwork and it was a breeze, more on this in Chapter 5).

Important Toll Road Tips

Always save the receipts when you travel the *cuotas* (toll roads) in Mexico. Why? Because when you pay a toll, you are automatically covered by the insurance provided by *Caminos y Puentes Federales*, and you will need that receipt if you ever need to make a claim.

According to *Baja Bound*, there is no deductible if you are driving a car, but there are deductibles if you are driving a bus, a small bus, or larger vehicles on the toll roads. The free insurance that comes with the toll road fee covers two scenarios: one if you are at fault, the other if you are not.

What's covered if you are at fault:

- Damage to the road.
- Damage to other vehicles, including the medical payments for occupants and pedestrians.
- Medical payments and funeral expenses for occupants of your vehicle.

The insurance will not cover damage to your vehicle if you are at fault!

What's covered if you are not at fault:

Damage to your vehicle, including towing expenses.

- Medical payments for occupants of your vehicle, including land ambulance to the nearest medical center.
- The above will be covered as a consequence of landslides, objects within the asphalt, holes, and substances that have been spilled on the road.

- If tires have been damaged, lights are broken, or glass breakage has occurred to the vehicle, the insurance will only cover the damage if it is due to the loose pavement on the road due to maintenance.

Toll Road Angels

The *Ángeles Verdes* (The Green Angels) regularly patrol Baja's *cuotas* (toll roads). These mobile mechanics offer free assistance in the case of a breakdown. Labor and towing are free, but vehicle owners would be on the hook for the cost of parts. If your vehicle breaks down, pull over to the side of the road and lift the hood to signal them. The Green Angels are also trained to give tourist information.

Although the Ángeles Verdes services on the toll roads are free, as with most services in Baja, tips are customary and always appreciated.

Know Before You Go: Handy Information About Traveling in Baja California, Mexico

- Many places, especially near the cities of Tijuana, Rosarito, and Ensenada, will accept dollars, but you will get a far better deal if you pay in pesos.

- Unlike in the U.S., many businesses do not accept credit cards, although most gas stations and grocery stores do. Therefore, you will need to carry more cash than at home.

- It's easy to get cash from ATM machines to avoid carrying too much, but be careful because ATM fees can add up quickly (see Chapter 9).

- While speaking the language will provide a richer experience, you can certainly get by without it in Baja. I know expats who have lived there for decades who barely speak a word of Spanish. Again, this is not recommended, but you can get away with it.

- No pumping your own gas, gas stations are full-service. Tips are appreciated.

- Mexico runs on tipping in general. An amount that means little to us can mean a lot to a poor working person who is bagging your groceries or cleaning your car windows. (More on tipping in Chapter 12.)

- Prices for things like hotels and campgrounds can vary vastly depending on where you go and who you know. Some of the expat-dominated high-end areas are starting to mirror U.S. rates. Well, maybe not quite, but they aren't cheap either.

- Local Facebook groups are invaluable for planning trips and finding things once you are there. Each city and town has one or more groups. Sometimes, even individual neighborhoods and camps (more on camps in Chapter 2) have their own groups. You can really get quite granular. Search for the areas you want to visit, join the groups, and you will get answers to most questions. (More on Facebook groups in Chapter 12.)

- Military checkpoints on the highways are a regular thing, so don't let them alarm you if you are stopped in one.

Military Checkpoints

Be aware that military checkpoints are a regular thing when driving in Baja. There are several known military checkpoints that are always active on various routes; others are short-term "pop-ups" and usually happen if law enforcement is looking for fugitives or in times of heavy tourists and visitor traffic, such as the Easter and spring break holidays or during the Baja 1000 off-road race week.

Heavily armed men in military fatigues stopping you on the road is intimidating to most Americans and Canadians, but don't let it

---

alarm you when you are stopped at a military checkpoint. I say *when*, not *if*, because if you drive for any time or distance in Baja, you *will* encounter a military checkpoint.

These are usually just cursory stops. The soldiers may ask to search your vehicle but usually won't (after seven years of clearing countless military checkpoints, it has yet to happen to me personally). They will ask where you came from and where you are going. They might ask to see your passport and/or visa or vehicle registration and proof of insurance. Have your proper immigration papers (see Chapter 5), and don't carry illegal items or suspicious amounts of cash, and you should be fine.

Flying Into Baja Norte

As of this writing, the only international airports in the northern part of Baja are in Tijuana and San Felipe. The latter is a stretch, as it's a tiny airport but as there are flights from other countries, it is considered an international airport. There has been noise about an international airport in Ensenada for over a decade, but nothing has materialized except that noise. I am sure it will eventually change as the region is exploding, but it hasn't yet.

Most Americans visiting Baja will find it easier and more affordable to fly into San Diego, walk over the border, and then take a bus or rent a car.

If you are flying into Baja from other countries, especially Central and South America, the Tijuana International Airport may be a better deal, so do some research.

Even private airports are in short supply. Private planes can use San Felipe's airport. It is also possible to get a permit to land at Ensenada's airport, which is part of the military air force base, but from talking to private pilots, it doesn't seem easy. I have yet to meet anyone who has actually done it, but I have met several pilots who deemed it not worth the trouble. But I have not researched it.

There are a few private airstrips in the remote areas of Baja south of San Felipe. Alphonsinas Resort (alphonsinas.com) on Gonzaga Bay is one. On the Pacific side you can find a private airstrip in Abreojos according to piloting friends, although that area is outside the scope of this book.

Like many things in Baja, joining local area Facebook groups can help give you the inside scoop (more info in Chapter 12).

Chapter 2: Where to Live in Northern Baja

Baja California, Mexico, is a long peninsula with more than 2,000 miles of coastline. You will encounter great options of places to go and places to live on either side of the Northern Baja peninsula, but they do offer distinctly different experiences.

Americans and Canadians will find thriving expat communities on both the Pacific and Gulf of California sides. In fact, some expats spend their winters in and around San Felipe, where the weather stays warm, and migrate over to the Rosarito/Ensenada side, where the ocean breezes off the Pacific keep things cool in the summer.

While I am in no way suggesting you communicate with or interact with only expats, having the resources of others who are in the same shoes, speak the same language, and have experience in the area can be invaluable. Especially if you need help or run into problems. (More about this in Chapter 12.)

Things to consider before choosing a locale

- How often will you cross the border and how close to it is your chosen location?

- How much do you need American foods, brands, stores, conveniences, etc.? If you answered a lot you will want to be near a larger city like Ensenada, or Tijuana.

- How secure is it? (More on this in Chapter 3.)

- What kind of climate suits you best? Baja has different climates that will appeal to different people. For instance, Canadian expat Thomas Rogan chose to live on a beach south of Ensenada because he said it fulfilled the two most important things he wanted in a locale: "Must not freeze, must not sweat." On the other hand, people who love the desert living of Arizona or New Mexico might prefer the Gulf Coast side of Baja.

So let's look at the pros and cons of both sides of the peninsula:

Pacific Coast pros:

- Easy access to and from San Diego, CA.
- Stays cool even in summer, no A/C needed.
- Great fishing.
- Lots of off-road races and motorsports.
- Surf (which can be a pro or con depending on your point of view).
- Decent-sized cities like Ensenada, Rosarito, and Tijuana, with every imaginable amenity you could want, plus lots of shopping, restaurants, nightlife, and entertainment options. You'll even find Costco, Sam's Club, Walmart, and most U.S. restaurant chains.
- Close to the Valle de Guadalupe wine country that offers world-class wines and fine dining. If you don't care about being on the ocean, this is another terrific place to set up a home base.

Pacific Coast cons:

- Colder in winter than on the other coast, but not cold by most people's standards. We are talking low 40s F. at worst, and that is extremely rare.
- It is more crowded and populated than the other side, which, depending on your point of view, can be a pro or a con.

- Mosquitos in summer can be brutal.

Gulf of California (formerly known as the Sea of Cortez) Coast pros:

- Warm but not hot in winter.

- Less crowded.

- Bathwater warm water in summer.

- Great fishing.

- Lots of off-road races and motorsports.

- Calm waters/no surf (which can be a pro or con depending on your point of view).

- Best of two worlds—this coast is where the desert meets the ocean.

Gulf of California Coast cons:

- Hotter than Hades for 6 months or more of each year.

- Less overall services, shopping, restaurants, entertainment, etc.

- Mosquitoes in summer can be brutal.

- Outside of San Felipe, you won't find much civilization other than a few small towns and tiny villages until you get to La Paz in Baja Sur, which can make road breakdowns extra stressful. You will also need to pack plenty of groceries as there will be no more supermarkets outside of San Felipe.

- Even in San Felipe, the largest city on this side of the peninsula, the largest supermarket is not nearly as large or well-stocked as what you'll find on the Pacific side. You also won't find the conveniences of Costco and other big city amenities like museums, live theaters, and other cosmopolitan city amenities.

Where to Live on the Pacific Side of Baja

You'll find both small and large towns and communities from San Diego to Ensenada on the Pacific side of the Baja Peninsula. If you venture south of Ensenada, there are still some small towns, but they begin to get sparser, and the expat communities in them are far smaller, which depending on your needs and views might be a good thing.

For the purposes of this book, Ensenada and its surrounding area will be the furthest point south we'll cover on the Pacific side.

Each area, and even each community within each area, has its own personalities and pros and cons. Of course, such things are highly subjective, so I advise you to check out different regions to find the one(s) you best vibe with. To be sure, there are more communities than just these, and more are developing all the time.. Below are some options and overviews to give you a general idea and places to start those explorations.

Tijuana

Directly over the border, Tijuana will be an option for those who need to frequently cross back and forth between Mexico and the U.S.

I will admit that I generally avoid TJ and head straight to the toll road south after crossing the border, even though there is a lot to see and do there. When I do visit, I go to the area I want to see, park, then explore. Driving around Tijuana's narrow, crowded streets is not for the faint of heart.

Be aware that, as with most border towns, Tijuana's crime rates tend to be higher than other places in the state. That aside, you will find world-class shopping and services in Tijuana and a thriving foodie scene with chefs and restaurants that are attracting international attention.

Most expats who opt to live in Tijuana will do so near the beach in the *Playas de Tijuana* neighborhoods.

Rosarito

Only about 15 minutes south of Tijuana, Rosarito offers great beaches and surfing, restaurants, and nightlife. There are also lots of festivals and events throughout the year. The demographic skews a bit younger than Ensenada further south, with lots of spring breakers and surfers coming through.

Rosarito provides a convenient beachside place to live that's close to the U.S. border, without quite being considered a "border town" like Tijuana. You'll find a thriving expat community there.

Puerto Nuevo

Twenty minutes or so south of Rosarito, lobster dinners are Puerto Nuevo's claim to fame. In reality, the area was fished out years ago and most of the lobsters are now imported, but tourists still flock here for the famous Puerto Nuevo lobster dinners.

There are beautiful beaches in this little town and its relatively close proximity to both Rosarito and Ensenada makes it a convenient home base.

How *Puerto Nuevo* Got Its Name

According to some Baja old-timers I once talked to at a locals' bar near La Bufadora, there never was a port at Puerto Nuevo. The name for this tiny seaside village came about back when there was little there besides a single restaurant. The old timers said that there used to be a big Newport cigarette billboard on the highway, which is how people would identify where to turn off for the restaurant. Newport/Puerto Nuevo. Get it? Apparently, the name stuck and the village has been known as Puerto Nuevo ever since.

Bajamar

If you enjoy luxury resort living, consider Bajamar, a seaside golf resort community south of Rosarito but north of Ensenada, giving you easy access to both.

This planned community is naturally more expensive than most other areas but offers many amenities other places don't, including a theater that hosts concerts from world-class entertainers, amazing beaches, restaurants, a spa, and, of course, great golf in spectacular oceanfront surroundings. For more information see golfbajamar.com.

Noise Alert

This is a personal observation after a lifetime of travel and of living in cities all over the world: cities in Baja are noisier than most. Yes, I know all cities are noisy. I lived in Los Angeles for decades, with police helicopters flying overhead every night and within the flight path of LAX. And while you won't often have helicopters or airplanes overhead in Baja cities, you will often (always?) have barking dogs, crowing roosters, neighbors' music and conversations, street vendors hawking their wares, sirens, traffic noise, and more, to deal with. At least until the wee small hours of the morning. And even then, expect it to start again at the crack of dawn.

I came to these conclusions after nights spent both in the hearts of Ensenada, Rosarito, and downtown San Felipe. The ease of walking to everything I needed in town was a big draw in all cases, but for me, it wasn't worth the noise factors in the long term. If you are a sound sleeper or if noise doesn't bother you, it might not be an issue. But if you opt to live in Baja cities, I suggest renting a hotel to try it out first.

Ensenada

I admit to having a soft spot for Baja's largest city, Ensenada. When I moved to Mexico, I made the small village of Punta Banda, just south of the city and on the way to La Bufadora, Baja's most famous natural tourist attraction, my Mexican home.

The greater Ensenada area features a large commercial and cruise ship port, lots of history, culture, entertainment, shopping, and restaurants, and fabulous festivals and special events throughout the year. If you are bored in Ensenada, it's your own fault.

When you leave the city proper heading south you'll find lots of agriculture. In fact, a lot of produce sold in the U.S. comes from here. Unlike a lot of areas in Mexico, vegetarians and even vegans won't have problems thriving here. And if you love seafood, the variety and quality available at Ensenada's *Mercado Negro* fresh seafood market boggles the mind.

While foreigners live all over the sprawling greater Ensenada area, those wanting the familiarity and security of living near other expats will find thriving mixed communities of gringos and locals in several places:

- North of town, especially in the upscale neighborhood of El Sauzal.
- In the Playas del Chapultepec area just south of town, including the Estero Beach resort.
- A little inland at the Baja Country Club planned community.
- In the new townhouse condominium neighborhoods that have sprung up immediately behind the Ensenada Costco store on the outskirts south of town.
- Further south of town in the small village of Punta Banda, the hillside villages of Esteban Cantú and Ramajal, and at the land's end point of La Bufadora a little farther down the road (these are all so close, I would consider them part of the same community).

Valle de Guadalupe

If you enjoy a fine wine and foodie culture in a high desert living setting, Mexico's premier wine country might be for you.

The Valle de Guadalupe, known to expats locally as "The Valle" (pronounced vahy-yay), is about 30 to 40 minutes inland from Ensenada. Its exploding growth is fairly recent. In 2000 there were only about 20 wineries. Today over 200 of all shapes and sizes call the Valle home.

Mexico's wines from this area are consistently racking up international medals and the region now produces almost 90% of all the wine that comes from Mexico.

Of course, with world-class wineries come world-class chefs and restaurants, not to mention artists and architects. The Valle reminds me of the Napa/Sonoma area of 30 years or more ago. But it's growing FAST!

Unfortunately, the downside of this is that the Valle is experiencing some growing pains and even more gentrification issues than other areas of Baja. The unprecedented growth, including hundreds of wineries, restaurants, hotels, and resorts - many of them with price tags rivaling their U.S. luxury counterparts - is making it more and more difficult for the local farmers and ranchers who have lived here for generations to keep up. Nonetheless and despite the growth, you will still find a lot of space in the Valle de Guadalupe.

Camps in Baja: They're NOT What You Think

When you look for housing to rent or buy in Baja, especially in the coastal areas, you will frequently encounter the word "camp" (or *campo*) regarding various neighborhoods. For instance, in the last seven years, I have lived in Campo 3, Campo La Jolla, and Campo Mar Azul (my favorite), all south of Ensenada. You will find other "camps" up and down both coasts of Baja.

It's important to realize when you hear the term that it doesn't

---

mean the same thing as it does in English. It means that this area or "camp" is under the control of one landlord, or family of landlords, who own the property. You can rent, or sometimes buy, homes in these camps, although even if you buy, you will usually still be leasing the land the house sits upon from the camp owner(s) (more on this in Chapter 8).

Each camp will offer its own amenities (or not), depending on the management of that camp. Some camps are better managed than others, something you get a better feel for once in Baja and once you start talking to others who live there.

Some camps might offer RV spaces. In many cases the homes themselves either are RVs or started out as an RV that subsequent generations have built upon and around. This can result in some interesting "Frankenhomes." Some are so well hidden, you would be hard-pressed to even find the original trailer. Others, not so much.

I suspect these places are called camps because that was their original purpose, a beachside vacation camp. Likewise, many of the beachfront homes were never built with year-round living in mind, although over the years that is what has come to pass.

These days housing in camps can run from mobile homes, to basic new or vintage houses, to modern luxurious McMansions. I talk more about all of this in Chapter 8.

Where to Live on the Gulf of California Side

For the purposes of this book, where I have purposely limited the locations to being no more than three hours from the border, San Felipe will be the main option for expats on the Gulf of California side.

Yes, there are camps further south within that range, but the vast majority of expats will want to be in or near San Felipe, as things get darn sparse going south for a long way after leaving this popular Baja destination. Eventually, you will hit Santa Rosalia and Mulegé, but you won't encounter another large(ish) city until La Paz, over 1100 miles away in the state of Baja California, Sur. If you want to live a remote off-grid coastal lifestyle, however, these areas present some amazing opportunities.

San Felipe

The town of San Felipe and the areas just north and just south of it are filled with lots of oceanside "camps" (see sidebar), housing developments, and RV parks, at all ends of the price and amenity spectrums. Thriving expat communities exist in and around San Felipe and this means built-in events and social activities galore for those looking to fit into their new community.

The town, which started as a small fishing village, also thrives on tourism, both from Americans and Mexicans, undoubtedly drawn by its endless sandy beaches. It's a popular snowbirding destination in winter, although high temps in summer drive some visitors away.

Heading further south out of town you will encounter lots of tiny mom-and-pop "camps." These won't have hookups if you are an RVer and even the sticks-and-bricks homes here are all off-grid. And don't expect any phone or internet service either, unless you carry satellite internet. The availability of Starlink in Baja has completely transformed the quality of life in these remote areas, where as recently as a few years ago, connectivity was almost non-existent.

What these primitive camps lack in modern-day infrastructure, they more than make up for in spectacular wild beauty. Imagine waking up to the sun rising over the crystal blue waters of the Gulf of California right outside your door. If you like to live far off the beaten path, this area of Baja offers some incredible opportunities.

Prices will be what you can negotiate with the camp owner. I have a friend in a camp where you can "own" your lot on the Bahia San Luis de Gonzaga shore on the Gulf of California, for about $1,200 a year. Bring your RV, or build on it. That's the long-term land lease rate in that camp and the lot is yours to do what you want with (within reason) for as long as you keep paying the rent.

Of course, you will have to truck everything in, set up off-grid power, satellite internet, and get water delivered from a local vendor (more on this in Chapter 11).

Inland Baja Norte: Mexicali and Tecate

Not as many American and Canadian expats settle in the state capital of Mexicali, or in the border town of Tecate, but some do. Perhaps that's because these inland cities lack the allure of the beaches or wine country. Nonetheless, they have a lot to offer including the fact that anywhere with fewer expats means a lower cost of living.

Despite being situated just over the border from Calexico, California, Mexicali has a reputation as being the safest border town in all of Mexico. It's also one of the most diverse cities in the country, where different cultures, traditions, and customs are readily visible.

Besides Mexican Nationals, Mexicali is home to people from all over the world, including Native Americans, Europeans, Africans, East Asians, Haitians, and Middle Easterners, along with a large Chinese population. In fact, it is well known throughout Baja that if you want great Chinese food, you go to Mexicali.

Living in the charming city of Tecate will also give you quick and easy access to the states, as well as the Valle de Guadalupe. One of 132 *Pueblos Magicos* or Magical Towns, in Mexico, the designation is awarded to communities that maintain their original architecture, traditions, history, and culture.

A lot of expats living on the Pacific side regularly opt to cross the border at Tecate, as this smaller crossing usually has less traffic and backup potential than the world's largest land border crossing in San Ysidro (immediately south of San Diego).

Chapter 3: Safety in Baja

When it comes to safety in northern Baja California, there is an enormous gap between public perception and reality. Sadly, many people are hesitant to even visit the region due to concerns over crime and violence, and these concerns are consistently elevated by sensationalized media coverage or isolated incidents that do not reflect the broader picture of what life here is actually like.

In reality, northern Baja California is generally as safe as many popular destinations around the world, including many US cities. But statistics, including those from the US government, would have you believe otherwise.

Theft and petty crime are the most common crimes expats encounter, and they are not uncommon. However, I have to say I have not personally experienced them in all my time in Baja. In the section on safety in public places, I'll go into more detail on how to protect yourself from petty crime.

But let's start by focusing on serious crimes, the kind that make people afraid to visit Mexico.

While it's always wise to stay informed and cautious, it's important to approach northern Baja California with the understanding that the fear outweighs the actual risk. No matter, that will never stop well-intentioned but ill-informed people from telling you how dangerous Baja is (see Chapter 4 for details).

One of the key distinctions between perception and reality is the fact that most of the crime in northern Baja, California is not directed at tourists or foreigners but is related to organized criminal and drug cartel activity.

Violent crime in the region tends to be concentrated in certain neighborhoods associated with illegal activities, usually far removed from the areas where most travelers and expats visit. The cartels are mercenary organizations and they have no desire to further bring down the weight and might of the United States government on themselves by targeting Americans. That would be bad for business.

Is there more to the story?

You will occasionally see sensational U.S. headlines about Americans being the targeted victims of violence in Mexico. The U.S. media paints accurate and gruesome accounts of grisly murders, but the alleged targeting of American tourists part of the story is almost always inaccurate.

I am in no way condoning the violence for any reason, BUT in almost all the cases since I have been living in Mexico, when these horrendous acts have occurred, there was far more to the story than was reported in the U.S. media.

While American media north of the border usually forgets the story after reporting the original sordid details of the crime, the Mexican press usually doesn't. There is almost always a cartel connection in these cases or some other deep-seated dispute that leads to the crimes.

Are the crimes immoral, horrific, and just plain wrong? Yes. One million percent. But what I am trying to convey is that they don't just happen out of the blue for no reason.

Like everywhere, there are exceptions, and evil people exist. But the point is, if you dig into these stories below the surface, you'll usually find more going on than the original U.S. reporting revealed.

Are You Safe in Mexico?

A comedic meme that regularly circulates in online expat groups asks the question, "Are you Safe in Mexico?" To answer accurately, the meme breaks down the replies:

- ***Do you intend to buy illegal drugs or interact with the cartels?*** If you answered yes, then no, you are not safe in Mexico. If you answered no, then you are as safe in Mexico as you are in the U.S.

- ***Do you intend to go out and get wildly drunk and act irresponsibly?*** If you answered yes, then no, you are not safe in Mexico. If you answered no, then you are as safe in Mexico as you are in the US.

- ***Do you intend to leave your resort?*** If yes, then you are as safe in Mexico as you are in the US. If not, then you are safer in Mexico than you are in the U.S..

That's pretty much on the mark. However, statistics tell a different story. There's no denying the fact that Baja has statistically high homicide and violent crime rates. The United States Department of State usually has some kind of travel advisory issued about Baja at all times. There has been one the entire time I have lived there, and I am certain long before that.

The one that's active as I write this (in November 2024) pretty much echoes what I have already advised in this chapter, albeit in a more fearful tone

Transnational criminal organizations compete in the border area to establish narco-trafficking and human smuggling routes. Violent crime and gang activity are common. Travelers should remain on main highways and avoid remote locations. Of particular concern is the high number of homicides in the non-tourist areas of Tijuana. Most homicides appeared to be targeted; however, criminal organization assassinations and territorial disputes can

result in bystanders being injured or killed. U.S. citizens and legal perma-
nent residents have been victims of kidnapping.

Visit this link to check out current travel advisories: travel.state.gov

Statistics aside, millions of people visit Baja California every year, the vast majority without incident, underscoring that while there are certainly safety concerns, they are not universal. Routine precautions—such as avoiding risky locations, especially after dark, not displaying valuables, and sticking to well-trafficked areas—can significantly reduce the likelihood of encountering problems.

Like in any other destination, including the United States, awareness and common-sense precautions go a long way toward ensuring safety.

Safety in Public Places in Baja

Petty theft and pickpockets are the biggest threats in public places where opportunistic thieves can take advantage of distractions and crowds. However, that's not a reason to miss all the fabulous festivals, celebrations, and events that Baja offers.

By following some simple but effective tips, you can minimize the risk of theft and enjoy public events with peace of mind. In fact, lately I feel safer at events in Mexico than I do in crowded U.S. places. With rare exceptions, random mass shootings are a uniquely American phenomenon that almost never happens in other countries, including Mexico.

- First and foremost, avoid carrying large amounts of cash or expensive items like jewelry, watches, or designer bags. Instead, carry only what you need for the day.

- Keep your wallet, phone, and credit cards in a secure, hard-to-reach place.

- A money belt or neck pouch that fits under your clothing can be an excellent option for carrying your passport, extra cash, and other valuables.

- If you prefer a bag, opt for one with a zipper and wear it across your body rather than slung over one shoulder.

- Keep your hand on your bag and be mindful of your surroundings, especially in busy markets, tourist spots, and public transportation hubs where pickpockets tend to operate.

- It's also a good idea to avoid displaying your phone or other valuables in crowded areas, particularly in places like Tijuana's busy streets or during popular festivals. If you need to take out your phone or camera for photos, do so quickly and avoid being distracted by your device for too long.

- Be aware of people who might approach you with unusual requests or who try to engage you in conversations that could distract you while an accomplice steals your belongings. Working in tandem, thieves often rely on creating confusion or diverting your attention to execute their schemes.

- Keep your wits about you and avoid intoxication.

Car Theft in Baja – It's Not What You Think!

Baja is not the best place to bring your flashy, expensive cars. Not only will they call unnecessary attention to yourself as a potential wealthy target, but also because the roads there, once off the *cuotas* or toll roads, will beat the crap out of a nice car.

A good, sturdy, utilitarian vehicle is far more practical. Extra points for four-wheel or all-wheel drive as it can come in handy in Baja, especially if you want to explore off the beaten path, and there is no end to amazing off-the-beaten-path places to explore including hot springs, a mountainous National Park, off-road trails, and more.

Surprisingly, though, fancy luxury cars are NOT the most common theft targets!

In 2024, Fox News 5 in San Diego reported that according to Rubén Alfredo Maximiliano Ramos, a prosecutor with the Baja Attorney General's Office, an average of 18 vehicles are stolen every day in Tijuana. That's lower than I would have guessed, it's an enormous, sprawling, densely populated city situated right on the border, and it has a high crime rate. Ramos said that thieves prefer anything made by Hyundai, Toyota, and Honda, along with Nissan Versa models.

Why these brands? Because they are common and easy to unload.

"There's no one gang or criminal organization doing this, most car thieves operate by themselves," Ramos continued. "What they do is try to unload or sell the cars immediately. Many times, these are addicts who are trying to get some quick money, or sometimes they use the stolen cars to commit other crimes."

He also states that shopping centers with large free parking lots tend to be the most problematic spots. Exercise caution accordingly.

Safety in the Home in Baja

Home burglaries are the second most common crimes expats may encounter. Once again, I can't say I have personally experienced this, but I know folks who have.

This type of crime is rarely organized and, like car thefts, is often the work of addicts looking for quick cash. Sadly, the U.S.'s meth problems are mirrored across the border in both the big cities and small villages. This can result in theft and burglaries. Of course, there is no way to 100% always prevent these occurrences any more than there is at home. But you can reduce the risks:

- Where you choose to live is important. Places with security are always preferable to those without—more on this in Chapter 8.

- Lots of exterior lights at night, or even better, motion sensor lights that will catch thieves off guard, are smart home accessories to install.

- Security cameras are another good idea. The police want to help, as do your neighbors, who are also trying to avoid getting ripped off. I have seen security camera footage in social media groups that has led to thieves being apprehended.

- Security alarms, whether with a service (only available in big cities) or just as a noisy deterrent, can't hurt. The same goes for cars. An alarm may or may not prevent a theft, but it definitely makes it more difficult and thieves are apt to move on to an easier target.

- Have secure locks and keep them locked when not there, at night, or whenever they don't need to be open. It never hurts to keep your vehicle locked, either.

- If you are inclined to get a dog, do so. So many rescues need homes in Baja, many canine-loving *gringos* tend to end up with multiple dogs. Even if it isn't specifically a guard dog, and there are many guard dog breeders and trainers in Baja, a barking dog (or any dog) is often an effective deterrent both at home and in your car.

- Many Americans (and Mexicans) maintain part-time vacation homes in Baja, leaving them empty and unattended for long periods. This invites break-ins. If this were my lifestyle, I would be sure to live in a neighborhood with full-time security and neighbors who look out for one another. Thankfully, both are common and easy to find in Baja.

Gun Ownership in Mexico

Mexico has restrictive gun laws. In fact, there is only one legally authorized firearms store in the entire country, the *Dirección de Comercialización de Armamento y Municiones* (DCAM), and it is far from Baja in Mexico City. Mexican citizens and legal foreign residents of Mexico may purchase firearms at the DCAM, provided they meet the necessary qualifications.

It is illegal to enter Mexico with a firearm without a permit from the *Secretariat of National Defense*. Mexican customs agents do not issue gun permits. This permit must be processed before you attempt to cross the border with any type of firearm or ammunition. Anyone entering Mexico with a gun or ammunition without a permit could face up to five years in prison.

In Mexico, legally owning and carrying a firearm are two different scenarios. You may own a registered firearm, which must be kept in the home. Still, to legally carry it, you need a license, which is typically reserved for police, military officials, some private security services, and specialized sporting participants.

One instance of the latter is an acquaintance who owned a business taking tourists on hunting trips in Baja. He was able to secure gun permits for his US tour participants for the period they were on the trip, but it did involve a lot of red tape and jumping through hoops..

Obviously, legal gun ownership in Baja is complicated at best and outside the scope of this book, but this gives you an overview.

Safety on the Road in Baja

Is driving in Baja safe? Generally speaking, yes. Especially on well-traveled and well-maintained routes like the toll roads. For the most part, if you drive carefully and safely, you will be fine. That said, there are some important things to be aware of.

Things to know about driving in Baja:

- Lack of Lighting: Once outside of a town, roads are not as well lit as they are in the States, if they are illuminated at all.

- Continuing from point 1, the lack of lighting can cause you to miss signs (see sidebar about my personal police encounters). Pay attention!

- When practical, it's a good idea to avoid driving at night (see below for details).

- The microbuses, privately owned public transportation, can be especially aggressive in traffic as time is money to them. Give them a wide berth, and be careful about them pulling out in front of you or cutting you off in traffic.

- Be aware of signs warning of *topes*, AKA speed bumps, in the road. Sometimes, *topes* placement makes sense. Other times there seems to be zero rhyme or reason for why they are there. But if you hit a *tope* at top speed, it's uncomfortable at best and painful, vehicle damaging, and expensive at worst.

- Stop signs here say *Alto*. They are smaller than stop signs in the States and are rarely illuminated (see sidebar about my experiences with law enforcement). As a side note, I don't know why they use the word for *high* or *tall* on the stop signs in Baja. When I told my multi-lingual Columbian Spanish tutor about this he was surprised and could make no sense of it as they don't call it that in South America. It appears this a regional Spanish linguistic difference, but know that an octagonal red sign that says *Alto* means stop!

- If you are stuck behind a slow-moving vehicle with its left turn signal seemingly stuck on, the driver probably does not intend to turn left anytime soon. Instead, they are trying to communicate that you should pass them when you can safely do so.

- Seeing trucks pass by filled with soldiers armed with automatic weapons is a common sight on Baja roads and highways. This can look scary and intimidating to unaccustomed Americans or Canadians, but it's nothing to be concerned about.

- Military checkpoints on the highways are a regular thing (see Chapter 1 for more details).

Is It Safe to Drive at Night in Baja?

The short answer is it depends. Usually, if you can avoid driving at night in Baja, that's a smart idea. People will tell you NEVER to do it, but that's a bit overboard. If you are in remote areas, or questionable areas of town, I would always advise not driving at night. But there are times when it isn't an issue:

- Within your small village, driving at night should not be a problem.

- The same goes for populous cities, providing you are avoiding bad neighborhoods.

- You should also be OK on the *cuotas*, but I would only go earlier in the evening when there are lots of other drivers on the roads and avoid them in the dead of night.

When it comes to driving at night in Baja, you always want to avoid remote areas and empty stretches of roads, not only because of potential crime like carjackers or banditos (more common in the remote areas south of what we are talking about in this book, although still uncommon), but also because of lack of lighting, potholes, *topes*, and the potential for turning a corner and running into livestock on the road.

So, while I do drive at night, I am selective about when and where I do it.

One more observation from experience that I am sure is largely due to the lack of lighting, but encountering cars driving with their high beams permanently on is an annoying but common occurrence in Baja. If you have night vision problems, this seemingly ubiquitous Mexican driving habit will likely exacerbate them.

Navigating Police Traffic Stops in Baja

Seeing the flashing lights of a police car in your rearview mirror is always stress-inducing. But traffic stops in Mexico, where you don't know what to expect and you may or may not speak the language, can be even more so. Those driving south of the border should be aware that traffic stops in Mexico are significantly different than in the United States.

If you are stopped for a traffic violation in Mexico, you will be asked for your driver's license, vehicle registration, and possibly proof of insurance. You will also be told what you did wrong.

Of course, in the U.S. you would then be issued a ticket that requires you to pay a fine or appear in court at a later date. Not so in Mexico! In Mexico, motorists follow the officer to the nearest police station then and there. Once at the station you can pay the fine or fight your case, should you feel the stop was unjustified. Unlike in the states, most road infractions are quite reasonable (usually about $20).

What I just described is how traffic stops in Mexico are supposed to work, according to the book. But in reality, they often don't work according to the book. However, there is another common scenario that you might find yourself in:

The *Mordita* Shake Down

Corruption happens everywhere in Mexico, but I like to call it "equal opportunity corruption" in that it is priced in such a way that anyone can play. I am not saying that you should ever attempt to bribe the police if you get pulled over by law enforcement. Doing so is illegal for both the person offering the bribe and the police officer accepting it.

That said, the practice is deeply ingrained in the culture and is done all the time. In fact, there are corrupt police who will stop drivers for no other reason than to extract a *mordita* or bribe. (The word in English means "small bite.")

If it makes you feel any better, it regularly happens to Mexican nationals as well as *gringos*. Take into consideration that the average cop in Mexico has to support his or her family on less than $15,000 a year, and you can understand *morditas'* commonality.

To be sure, locals on the community social media boards hate it when anyone pays a *mordita*, as they say it just continues the practice. That may well be true. Yet I suspect many of the loudmouths do it when they get stopped. In the fifty-plus years that I have been traveling to Baja, absolutely nothing has changed regarding *morditas*. Likewise, for all practical purposes, the practice doesn't show any signs of stopping.

Again, I present this strictly for informative purposes. I am not saying you should ever attempt to bribe a law enforcement officer. But I would be remiss if I did not inform you about *morditas*.

My Personal Experiences with Traffic Stops in Mexico

The first time, it was dusk, and it was on my first trip to Punta Banda in about 20 years. A lot had changed. While driving my Class B motorhome, I missed a small *Alto* (stop) sign partially hidden behind some bushes. I ran the stop sign and nearly t-boned a cop coming the other way. Of course, I got pulled over, and rightfully so.

While I was apologizing profusely for my error to one officer out the driver's side window, my male traveling companion was talking to another on the passenger side. The next thing I knew, we were on our way. When I inquired how, my friend informed me he asked the officer if he could "pay the fine here instead of going to the station" and took $20 out of his wallet. The cop took the bill and told us to drive on. I considered it a bargain, considering my error.

The second time I was stopped, it was a pure *mordita* shakedown and nothing more. We were in heavy traffic. I was not speeding and, in fact, could not speed. Nonetheless, I was pulled over. The officer claimed he stopped me because I was on my phone. I explained that I was not on my phone and that the car had a complete hands-free phone system in its dash. I had no need to ever hold my phone.

OK, that didn't work. Next, he claimed he stopped me because my dogs were loose and not in cages in the car. I have since learned this is technically the law (and it is being enforced more these days). However, on that day, I was not having it. I had regularly seen passels of kids and dogs loose in the back of open pickup trucks, and the police never bat an eye, let alone stop those vehicles. I was hungry, tired, and not in a good mood when I told him, "Enough of this. I will go to the station."

That stopped everything. He did not know what to do. I don't think anyone had ever called him on it before.

He nervously told me to lead the way, and he would follow me. I said I didn't know where the station was, so I would follow him. We took off driving slowly—very slowly—about 20 mph until we came to a stop sign about a quarter-mile down the road. He exited his car, returned to mine, and simply said, "Go home."

And that was the end of it. So, if you think you are in the right, it can pay to politely challenge a *mordita* shakedown.

Remember, the goal of the police officer in most mordita situations is to make a little extra cash without getting caught and with minimum hassle. He is looking for frightened people willing to pay to go about their day. He does not want to explain to his commanding officer that he was trying to shake down a gringo.

What Happens If the Police Are Criminals?

I have never experienced true thuggery at the hands of Mexican police, but I know it sometimes happens. Every now and then a tale will filter onto the ex-pat community boards on Facebook.

It's not common, but when it happens, it is almost always in remote areas far outside of the scope of this book's coverage. It's not pretty. Police have been known to steal cash, cameras, jewelry, and other valuables.

However, even in these stressful situations, some who have stood their ground have made it stop. Taking out a cell phone to film the encounter often does the trick. But if you find yourself in this type of unfortunate encounter, you will need to judge the mood and danger of the situation and your location yourself.

One thing to know is that these crimes are usually committed by lower-ranking officers. Getting caught doing them, like shaking down people for *morditas* (see separate sidebar), can cost them their jobs. They do not want to get caught.

Chapter 4: The Downsides of Baja

As wonderful as most of us expats think it is, living in Baja, California, Mexico, is definitely not for everyone, and this chapter will go into why not, along with how to evaluate if it is for you.

One of the first hurdles many Americans and Canadians face is the constant concern from family and friends back home. Loved ones often harbor fears about safety, influenced by sensationalized media reports or a general lack of understanding about life south of the border. Crime and cartel violence are often highlighted in the news, leading to anxiety among family members who worry for their loved ones' well-being.

No matter how long you live in Baja and how many years (decades) of experience you have there, you will still encounter well-intentioned but ill-informed friends and relatives telling you how dangerous and awful Mexico is. It sounds silly that someone who has never been to, let alone lived in, a place would tell someone who does live there what it is like, but it happens constantly. And it is maddening.

When you are in the planning stages of a Baja move, you will quickly lose track of the number of people who will tell you that you are crazy. This pressure from loved ones has prevented several people I know from ever making the move, even though they wanted to, and they personally knew better.

That's a shame because living in Baja is nothing like what these ignorant people, the sensationalized media, or the government crime stats portray. Find more details in Chapter 3. But the fact is, there is absolutely nothing, and I do mean NOTHING, you can do or say to convince certain people that you are perfectly sane and safe living in Baja. So don't even try. These people should not go to Mexico. It's not for them.

Baja is Not for Everyone

Let's face it, we Americans are spoiled. In the U.S., within reason, we can pretty much get anything, anytime, anywhere.

Take an inventory and be honest with yourself. Are you spoiled? Do you love and need the pampering most Americans take for granted? Do you lose your temper if the DoorDash order is late or if the gardeners suddenly don't show up on their scheduled day?

If the answer is yes, then Baja is probably not for you unless you are wealthy by both country's standards. In that case, anything is possible.

The pristine, ultra-reliable infrastructure of the United States doesn't always carry over to life in Northern Baja. Power outages, inconsistent water supplies, and spotty internet connections are inconveniences that can lead to frustration. I am not saying these things are everyday occurrences, but they do happen from time to time.

Furthermore, it's not all neat and pretty. Like many countries, it's not unusual to find a big expensive house next to a tiny rundown one. There may or may not be landscaping. Your favorite restaurant might be housed in a building that's barely a shack. Some of the homes for sale or lease have been built around RVs as many beach properties started as vacation camps and have morphed into permanent homes through the decades.

Also, when someone is expected to be there for a service appointment, other things can and do take precedence when necessary. While the Mexican people are some of the most hard-working in the world, the culture is different than in the U.S. where your job often owns you (and I think this difference is a good thing). Family always takes priority in

Mexico. So, if your housekeeper's kid is sick, she won't be coming to work. Or if a family emergency came up, your favorite little breakfast spot might be unexpectedly closed that day.

Experienced expats shrug, say "Viva Mexico," and move on. But these disruptions can feel like an ongoing struggle for those used to a life of constant privilege, comfort, and convenience.

That said, life in Baja is not super inconvenient, either. But it is different. If you have an adventurous spirit and the ability and temperament to embrace the unexpected, you might be a good fit for Baja.

What are these inconveniences? Here are some common examples:

- No ordering online and getting it delivered the next day. Amazon Prime boxes are starting to pop up in Baja and Amazon even offers some home delivery, but you must order through Amazon, Mexico. Friends report mixed results in getting those orders, something I expect to improve with time, but as of this writing, it is not as reliable as it is in the States.

- There's no at-home mail delivery at all.

- Utilities are less reliable (more in Chapter 11).

- Drinking water does not come out of the tap, and the water that does come out of the tap is often distributed differently than in the states (more in Chapter 11).

- Businesses may or may not keep regular hours, and this can change at any time without any notice.

- Finding reliable customer service and workers such as auto repair people, handypersons, and housekeepers can be challenging. To be fair, this can also be a challenge in the US. When you find someone good, you reward them well and keep them!

- You can't stream the same media that you can in the States. Different companies have different licensing agreements in international markets. Just because you can stream certain movies or series at home does not necessarily mean you can watch them in Baja. Using a virtual private network (VPN) connection can sometimes help you get past this, but not always.

- Grocery stores may or may not carry the same brands or products you are used to, although they regularly do carry many of them.

- If you need to cross the border frequently, it can become a major pain-in-the-you-know-where. There are tips to alleviate border stress in Chapter 12, but at certain times, there is nothing you can do about it.

What Isn't Cheaper in Baja?

It's true that most goods and services are less expensive in Baja than in the United States. Some goods that are produced locally or specifically tailored to the Mexican market may be priced similarly or higher than in the U.S., depending on supply and demand, but most things cost less.

Most but not all. Some things tend to cost more in Mexico. Let's explore the things that are not such a great deal, financially speaking:

Fuel: As in most non-US countries, fuel in Mexico generally costs more. How much more will depend on where you came from in the U.S. When I first moved to Mexico in 2017, fuel costs were slightly higher than in my home state of California, one of the most expensive states in the union for fuel prices. When fuel prices in the U.S. shot up a few years back, and California gas prices went north of $6.00 a gallon, prices in Mexico were slightly less than in California.

As of this writing they are about even or slightly more again. But that's compared to California. At about $4.91 a gallon (as of this writing), Mexico's fuel prices are significantly higher than in most states. Yes, prices change, but fuel prices don't change much in Mexico because they are regulated and stabilized by the government. Likewise, expect to spend more on fuel in Baja. One good thing, however, you won't have to pump it yourself as all stations are full service.

Electronics: Most electronics are imported and have hefty tariffs imposed on them. Likewise, electronics can cost consumers more in Mexico, so these are good items to bring with you when you move. It's not always significant. Costco stores in Tijuana and Ensenada often offer electronics prices that are on par with those in the States. But usually, electronics are more expensive in Baja.

Some Imported Goods: Due to import tariffs and taxes, certain imported goods, especially cars and luxury items, can be more expensive in Baja.

Pet Food and Pet Supplies: Overall, Mexico is a poor country, and pets are a luxury many people cannot afford. Likewise, pet food and pet supplies are often more expensive than in the U.S., and there tends to be less availability and variety. The good news is that groceries are so inexpensive here, you can make healthier homemade dog food using natural ingredients like chicken, beef, and organ meats. It's far less expensive than buying processed pet foods, far healthier for your pet, and with a slow cooker or Instant Pot, the process is super easy.

Half and Half, Cream, and Ice Cream: You'll be hard-pressed to find half and half in Northern Baja outside of *gringo* neighborhoods, and even there, it's only available in shelf-stable packaging and available all the time. Cream is available at well-stocked supermarkets, but it's somewhat pricey, as is decent ice cream. On the other hand, milk in all varieties of fat and lactose content is no problem, as are a variety of vegan milk substitutes.

My #1 Least Favorite Thing About Baja

By far, my personal least favorite thing about Baja is the proliferation of sick, injured, and starving street dogs. I am a dog lover and street dogs are a heartbreaking and sad fact of life here. While many Mexicans treat their pets like valued family members, many do not, and they are looked at more like simple property or are

---

strictly working animals. It is a cultural difference. Poverty, no doubt, also plays a huge part. Spaying and neutering are not the norm here, and a whole lot of dogs end up living on the streets.

I always keep kibble in my car. While the little guys can usually scrounge enough to survive at the taco stands, the bigger dogs have more trouble.

Things are slowly changing, thanks in no small part to the tireless work of rescue organizations like Ensenada's *Los Adoptables*. The angels at this organization and others like it work miracles, healing dogs and cats that seem beyond hope, and finding them loving homes. They also hold low- and no-cost spay/neuter clinics and educate the public, starting at the grammar school level, about the importance of spaying and neutering and properly caring for animals.

Los Adoptables is a worthy place for animal lovers to volunteer if you move to the Ensenada area. They also hold fun fundraising social events and run a year-round *segunda* store (second-hand or thrift shop). Find more information here: losadoptables.org

P.S: If you are a horse lover, be sure to check out my friends' Baja equine rescue, *Tina Jo's Promise*. tinajospromise.org

PART II
Moving to Baja Logistics and Practicalities

Moving to another country, even one as easy to move to as the northern part of Baja, Mexico still involves many logistical details that cannot be overlooked. Consulting this section of the book should help keep you on track.

Chapter 5: Visas and Immigration

Before applying for temporary or permanent residency in Mexico, I recommend first visiting as a tourist by purchasing an FMM card (*Forma Migratoria Múltiple*), which will allow you to legally remain in the country for up to 180 days (6 months). You can get your FMM card online (recommended) at inm.gob.mx or in person at some border crossings. Either way, you will need to stop at the border to get the card stamped when entering Mexico.

Yes, you can qualify for and set up temporary or permanent residence first, but I always recommend that people try things out first before going through the hassle and expense. If you like Baja life, you can tackle these issues down the road. If you don't, you will not have invested too much time or money, and you can simply go home.

Requirements for Obtaining an FMM Card

- You must hold a valid and current passport or card passport in accordance with international law regulations.

- If your country of citizenship requires it (and the U.S. does not), the passport must have a valid unexpired visa.

- You must complete the information needed in the request for the FMM as it appears in your passport.

- The FMM does NOT allow you to work in Mexico, only visit.

- As of this writing (Nov. 2024), an FFM card costs $717 pesos (about $43 U.S. dollars).

Get your FMM card!

I know of many expats who never bother with obtaining an FMM card, or residency visas for that matter. Some have gotten away with it for decades, probably because they rarely leave home. Don't do this! Besides just being wrong, the Mexican police can and do check these things and crack down on them from time to time, and you never know when your luck will run out on your way to the grocery store.

As I was writing this chapter (in November 2024), the following message appeared in the San Felipe area Facebook group:

"Get your FMM! Checkpoint just before San Felipe, southbound, checking every *gringo* vehicle. No FMM, return to border."

It's rare, but the police have even been known to go door to door in expat neighborhoods, checking for valid immigration visas. This typically only happens when tensions between the usually amicable relations with the U.S. rise, but with the current political climate, I think we can expect more of that.

Bottom line, get your FMM card!

Temporary Residency and Permanent Residency in Mexico

Temporary and permanent resident visas allow you to stay in Mexico longer, forever, in the latter case. Know that you do not necessarily need one before the other. If you qualify for permanent residence from the start, you can skip the temporary residence visa altogether. If you don't, getting a temporary residence visa will help you qualify for permanent residence in four years, regardless of your income level.

Temporary Residence

The Temporary Resident Visa allows individuals to stay in Mexico for more than 180 days but no longer than four years. It is approved for one year and then subsequently renewed for one to three additional years.

Just like with a permanent residency visa, you will begin the process of obtaining a temporary residence visa at a Mexican consulate on the U.S. side for the border. (If you are married to a Mexican citizen, or your family ties include a Mexican citizen, there may be exceptions to this rule.)

As a temporary resident, you may apply for a work visa in Mexico, although don't count on this to earn your living for reasons to be discussed in Chapter 9.

Both temporary and permanent residence visas come with minimum financial requirements. The Mexican government, rightfully so, wants to ensure that new immigrants do not become a burden on the system. The amount of money needed to qualify is based upon a multiple of Mexico's minimum wage and goes up every year. This is making it more difficult for many people to qualify, however, there are sometimes ways around this that we will discuss below.

The most common way, if you can qualify for temporary residence, is to remain in the country for four years. You can then apply for permanent residence, even though you may fall under the required income thresholds. Of course, you must first qualify for temporary residence (more below).

Permanent Residency

Permanent residency is the next step for those who wish to remain in Mexico indefinitely. If you qualify for permanent residency, it can be the first and only step necessary. In other words, you do not necessarily need to be a temporary resident first, although this route makes the most sense for many people who can't meet the permanent residency income requirements.

In addition to those who qualify financially, permanent residency visas are typically granted to individuals who have held temporary residency for at least four years or who can demonstrate strong ties to Mexico. The process for applying for permanent residency is easiest for retirees but can also be granted because of family connections or business interests within the country.

Once granted, permanent residency offers the benefit of never needing to renew visas or temporary permits ever again. It also allows you to work in Mexico without restrictions and gives you access to other benefits available to Mexican citizens, such as public healthcare.

As a permanent resident, you have almost every right that a Mexican citizen has, with these exceptions:

- The right to vote.
- The right to run for public office.
- The right to own land in your name in the "restricted zone," within one hundred kilometers (sixty-one miles) of the international border and fifty kilometers (thirty-one miles) of the seacoast. This effectively means all of Baja. (Learn more on how foreigners can own land in Baja in Chapter 8.)

Of course, you could opt to become a naturalized citizen of Mexico, but this is outside the scope of this book. For our purposes, we assume you will keep your U.S. or Canadian citizenship.

An Unofficial Residency Card Benefit

According to my Mexican attorney, Carlos Victorica Reyes, if you are ever stopped by the police, use your temporary or permanent residency card for your ID along with your driver's license. Carlos says the police are more likely to have respect for gringos who live there and support the community than they do for transient visitors.

Financial Requirements for Temporary or Permanent Residence

There are four ways to qualify for residency in Mexico using your financial means/assets:

- By demonstrating you have a minimum *monthly net income*.
- By holding a *minimum balance* in personal savings/investments.
- By owning a house in Mexico with a specified *minimum value* (I talk more about owning property in Baja in Chapter 8).
- By making a specified capital investment in a Mexican company.

You must qualify financially with the minimum amount required under only one of the above categories. In other words, you cannot mix means/asset types. Also, if you own a house in the United States, its value is not counted as an asset for the purpose of immigrating to Mexico.

The amounts required change each year. As of 2024, for temporary residence, you must show six months of bank accounts proving you made at least $4,350 U.S. ($6,160 Canadian) per month in after-tax income. Make that $7,300 ($10,267 Canadian) a month for a permanent residence visa. As a side note, you could live extremely well in Baja on any of these incomes.

Alternatively, you can show qualifying savings/investments account balance(s) totaling at least U.S. $73,200 ($102,671 Canadian) over the last 12 months for temporary residence or $293,000 ($410,685 Canadian) for permanent residence. Note that the totals must not fall below the minimum amount required at any time during those 12 months.

I asked attorney Carlos Victorica Reyes about if or how the requirements change in the case of married couples. He said that for couples, the financial requirements would equal one and a half times the amount of a single person. So in other words, instead of needing to make $7300 U.S. dollars a month to qualify for permanent residence, a couple would need to show an income of $10,950.

Yowza! That is a lot of money for most people. We will talk about exceptions to the income requirements, below.

Carlos also said that it is much easier and simpler to immigrate to Mexico as a "retired person," even if you do plan to continue to work remotely or maintain your U.S. business once living in Mexico. Younger people who meet the income requirements can also immigrate, but according to Carlos, it is a bit more complicated and entails explaining the situation to the consulate when applying for temporary residence.

Do You Need a Mexican Immigration Attorney?

Technically, no. You can complete all your immigration applications yourself and complete the process without an attorney's help. You can find detailed instructions on how to do so online. However, a good Mexican immigration attorney can certainly streamline the process and save you a lot of wasted time.

The online expat boards are filled with stories from people who neglected to cross a "t," dot an "I," or forgot some other little detail, which caused their applications to be kicked out. Then, they had to start the entire immigration process all over again.

A good immigration attorney can tell if you will qualify in advance and can sometimes help you find ways to qualify when you didn't think you could. So, if you can't qualify for the income requirements, and according to attorney Carlos Victorica Reyes who specializes in immigration and other services for expats living in Baja, most people can't, a consultation with a good immigration attorney might reveal other avenues to pursue.

You'll hear a lot about Carlos in this chapter, as I could not have written it as well without his invaluable guidance, as even the Mexican government website can be confusing when it comes to legal issues.

When I applied for (and received) permanent residency, Carlos did everything, including making my appointments at the Mexican consulate in Calexico, California. All I had to do was show up on time, hand over the packet of papers he had prepared, answer a few questions, get photographed and fingerprinted, and that was it. A few weeks later, after one more brief interview on the Mexican side of the border, I got my permanent resident card.

As far as I am concerned, it was money well spent to not have to worry about anything or go through the bureaucracy involved myself. If you want to contact Carlos, find his website at expatguardian.com.

Conversely, if you have a lot of time and not a lot of money, you can certainly opt to do your temporary or permanent residency visas yourself. Many people do.

Exceptions to the Minimum Income Residency Requirements

There are ways around the minimum income requirements depending on your circumstances. There may be more than what's listed below, which is where a good immigration attorney can help, as I am definitely NOT an attorney on either side of the border. Nonetheless, here are some of the most common ways:

- **Marry a Mexican:** Marrying a Mexican citizen will allow you to permanently remain in the country. And yes, gay marriage is legal in Baja and all of Mexico. I am in no way suggesting that you should marry a Mexican for this purpose alone and doing so would be illegal. However, if your inter-country romance is going well, you just might want to pop the question.

- **Have a Child:** Just as above, I am in no way suggesting you have a child for this sole purpose, but according to Carlos, just as in the U.S., having a child in Mexico allows you to permanently stay in the country.

- **Family Ties:** A Mexican spouse or close family member, such as a parent, can help you qualify for residency without income requirements.

- **Invitation from a Public or Private Institution:** If you can show an original letter from a public or private organization or institution of "renowned integrity" inviting you to participate in a non-renumerated activity in a Mexican territory, you may be able to qualify for temporary residency. Scientists, biologists and environmentalists working along the coasts often qualify, as do church group members who build housing for the poor, and medical personnel who offer services to Baja's orphanages and underprivileged communities.

- **Mexican Real Estate:** Owning real estate in Mexico of a designated value can fulfill your financial requirements. The value amounts change, but as of this writing, the real estate must exceed $4,289,820 Mexican pesos ($210,875 U.S. or $299,108 Canadian) in value. Learn more about owning real estate in Baja in Chapter 8.

- **Investing:** Investing a designated amount in a Mexican corporation or partial ownership worth a designated value can also fulfill your financial residency requirements.

- **Amnesty:** Carlos said this is a little-known residency qualifying exception (I told you a good immigration attorney can help). If you were in Mexico before December 31, 2022, even if it was just for a quick weekend trip, and your passport and FMM card prove it, you are eligible for temporary residence for up to 4 years without any income requirements. Note that the amnesty program does not apply to cruise ship passengers who embark for a few hours before returning to the ship, as these passengers enter the country with a slightly different visa. Carlos said you could probably mount a legal challenge to the cruise ship exception, but it would be too costly and time-consuming to be worth it. However, if you arrived in Mexico by car, by air, or by boat other than a cruise ship, check with a Mexican immigration attorney for details on how to apply for temporary residence.

Chapter 6: Healthcare in Baja

When it comes to healthcare in Baja, expats have several options (or combinations of options):

- Keep your U.S. insurance and travel across the border for care.
- Buy a health insurance policy that covers you in Mexico.
- Pay for health expenses out of pocket.

Paying cash for healthcare in Mexico is common because unlike in the U.S., the fees are actually affordable. If you need care, simply go to a doctor. To give you an idea, an Ensenada neighbor recently paid about $30.00 for a doctor's appointment with a general practitioner.

Many expats keep their U.S. insurance but for simple things, just pay out of pocket to see a local doctor rather than hassle with crossing the border.

Medical care in Baja is so affordable that it has even become a medical tourism destination, especially for dental work, cosmetic surgeries, and alternative therapies often not available in the United States. Clinics with English-speaking staff are set up for medical tourists in or near border towns – for instance, you will find a large assortment of them in Tijuana. You will discover that you can have the work done, have a nice vacation, and have money left over compared to what the work alone would cost in the U.S. And if you already live in Baja, it's that much easier to access these services anytime without having to travel to a border town.

To be sure, if something serious requiring surgery or long-term care happens, things can and do get expensive in Mexico. So, while it's easier to get by without insurance in Mexico than it is in the States, it is always prudent to have it.

An internet search will help you find health insurance companies that cater to expats. You can also find a Mexican insurance agent once in Baja who can help you with a policy to cover your health care there.

Of course, keeping their U.S. insurance and traveling over the border works for many expats, especially those in proximity to San Diego.

National Medical Care

If you decide to stay in Mexico and become a legal permanent resident, you will qualify for the same national health care that Mexican citizens get. The quality of such care is debatable, but you nonetheless are covered for ambulance and emergency care, as well as many other conditions.

Judging from the experience of my Canadian expat neighbor Renata Rogan who recently had hip replacement surgery at one of Ensenada's public hospitals, it's not convenient, and if you go this route you can expect a lot of bureaucracy, red tape, and long waits. She said if you have a private doctor who works at the hospital, as she did, the process may be somewhat expedited.

She reported that the care at the public hospital was adequate but basic at best, and certainly unlike what most Americans and Canadians are accustomed to. For instance, patients are required to bring their own pillows and blankets. She also said that even by hospital food standards, the food was terrible, and nothing is available between scheduled meals, not even water. Likewise, patients are encouraged to pack food and drinks from home.

Nonetheless, the surgery was successfully completed at virtually no cost to Renata, save the price of the actual hip replacement part itself, which was not covered.

When I asked if she would do it that way again, Renata admitted she would probably opt for a private hospital instead and cited the positive experience a mutual friend had getting a knee replacement at a private hospital in Baja that more closely mirrored a U.S. hospital experience.

Pharmacies in Baja

You'll find an abundance of pharmacies catering to both locals and tourists in Baja. These pharmacies range from well-established, legitimate businesses to smaller, less reputable establishments and it is important to understand the difference.

Legitimate pharmacies in Northern Baja are clean, well-organized, and staffed by licensed pharmacists. They are often affiliated with national or regional chains, such as Farmacias Similares, or Farmacias Roma. Similarly, the pharmacies at retail chains such as Costco or Walmart carry an equal amount of trust.

Key Characteristics of Legitimate Pharmacies:

- Clearly displayed business licenses and certifications.
- Transparent pricing with labeled products.
- Consistent stock of recognized brands and generic medications.
- Pharmacists on-site to answer questions and verify prescriptions.
- Some of these pharmacies may also have adjacent clinics where visitors can consult a doctor for a nominal fee, enabling them to obtain prescriptions for medications that require them under Mexican law.

In contrast, smaller, independent "sketchy" pharmacies may prioritize profit over customer safety. These establishments often cater to tourists looking for easy access to medications without a prescription, but their practices can be questionable. Purchasing from these pharmacies carries risks, including counterfeit, expired, and sometimes dangerous medications, and potential legal complications.

Key Warning Signs of Sketchy Pharmacies:

- No licensed pharmacist on-site.
- Unlabeled or improperly stored medications.
- A focus on selling controlled substances or high-demand drugs.
- Aggressive marketing tactics or offers to "prescribe" medications without a medical evaluation.

U.S. Prescription Drugs That Do Not Require Prescriptions in Mexico

Many medications that require a prescription in the United States are available over the counter in Mexico. Common examples include:

- Birth control pills
- Erectile dysfunction medications
- Blood pressure medications
- Cholesterol-lowering medications
- Diabetes medication, including many types of insulin
- Heartburn and GERD medications
- Some pain medications, such as Tramadol
- Antidepressants such as Celexa, Wellbutrin, and a variety of SSRIs
- Steroid medications such as Prednisone
- Anti-parasitics like Ivermectin

These medications are usually much cheaper than in the United States and are available at most pharmacies.

Drugs That Do Require Prescriptions in Mexico

While Mexico has more relaxed rules for many medications, certain drugs still require a valid prescription. These include:

- Most antibiotics
- Opioid painkillers such as Percocet, Oxycodone, Vicodin
- Anxiety medications like Xanax, Klonopin, Ativan, and other benzodiazepines
- Asthma inhalers, like Albuterol, Breo, and others
- ADD and ADHD medications, like Ritalin, Strattera, and Vyvanse.

Mexican pharmacies will ask for a prescription for these medications, especially in legitimate establishments. In many cases, the on-site physician (see above) can write that prescription. Some sketchier locations may sell these drugs without one, but doing so is illegal and can result in legal consequences for both the buyer and seller.

Medical Marijuana Use in Baja

Mexico's current relationship with medical marijuana and cannabis in general is complicated and confusing, as it is most everywhere in the world.

It is illegal to enter Mexico with cannabis, and yes, that does include state-legal medical marijuana, regardless of whether or not you have a medical marijuana card at home. This is not to say that it isn't regularly done. But know that if you do get caught, it can become a serious incident.

A few years back, Mexico's Supreme Court declared it legal for Mexican citizens to possess and even grow personal use amounts of cannabis. That was during the COVID epidemic, and the rules were never clarified especially concerning sales and commerce, so you won't find any legal dispensaries in Baja. Also, the ruling only technically applies to Mexican nationals, not visitors. The issue has more or less been kicked down the road ever since.

CBD is readily commercially available; however, just as in the U.S. CBD market, the quality of the products you'll find are often of questionable integrity. *Caveat emptor* on both sides of the border on CBD.

Despite the murky legal status of the plant and its derivatives, responsible, discreet cannabis use is prevalent, especially in the retiree-filled expat communities. Once you settle in and make friends, procurement won't be a problem. Just like in the US before the legalization of medical and recreational cannabis in many states, someone always knows "a guy." Some expats even maintain discreet secret gardens at their homes.

Is any of this legal and without risk? Absolutely not. No more than it is in certain conservative U.S. states. Know that I am in no way advising you to participate in illegal activity on either side of the border.

So, when people ask me if marijuana is legal for expats in Mexico, the answer is no. But is it common? You betcha!

Chapter 7: Kids and Pets

It's outside the scope of this guide to go into a lot of detail on the topic of raising children in Mexico. That said, bringing your children to Baja and raising them there, if you are financially able to do so, can provide some advantages:

- As the cost of living is lower, your family will have more money for other things.

- You offer your kids the ability to become bi-lingual at a young age when learning languages is easiest. If they learn Spanish early enough, they'll speak like natives and won't even have an American or Canadian accent!

- Your children will have opportunities to learn an appreciation for another culture in ways that children in the U.S. never can.

Of course, education will be the biggest concern for most parents. Expats will find both public and private school options in Baja. Public schools are taught entirely in Spanish, which may or may not be an issue depending on your child's age and language abilities. Of course, you will need to be permanent residents to enroll your kids in public school.

For private schools, you will need to be near a larger city like Ensenada or Tijuana, but if you are near a good private school, your child can get a high-quality bilingual education.

Homeschooling is another education option, and with today's technology it has never been easier. You can probably even afford to hire a tutor if you prefer not to do the teaching yourself. Of course, the downside to this is the lack of social interaction.

I have to say that while I have come across a number of expat families who have migrated to Baja, the practice is not nearly as common as it is for retirees and childless singles and couples. But it is entirely feasible to raise your expat kids in Baja.

Bringing Your Pets to Baja

The US government just made crossing the border with pets a little more complicated than it used to be, but it's still not all that difficult. Going into Mexico remains simple providing you carry proof of vaccines and a health certificate from your vet.

Until recently, my friends and I regularly crisscrossed the border with our dogs, but with all the new rules, we now leave them at home in Baja unless it is a long trip. You can easily find dog walkers and pet sitters at reasonable rates. Like all services, your local neighborhood's Facebook group will be invaluable.

The Rules for Bringing Dogs and Cats Into Baja, Mexico

The official government rules say the pet must be in a carrier, and many local municipalities have this rule, too. However, it seems only to be selectively enforced - for instance, see the sidebar on my police stop experiences in Chapter 3. That said, chatter in the expat social media groups would indicate that it is starting to be enforced more frequently than when I moved to Baja in 2017, so keeping a carrier or pet seatbelt restraint system in your car is a good idea.

The rules also state that you must have a health certificate and vaccine records for your dogs and cats. I have always carried these, although I have never been asked for them in practice. Nonetheless, I would not dream of crossing the border without them, just in case.

Other animals have different rules, so consult the Mexican government website if you are traveling with animals other than cats and dogs.

Bringing Pets Into the United States from Mexico

It used to take the same requirements to get dogs back in the U.S. as it did to get them into Mexico. However, the USDA instituted new rules in 2024.

To bring a dog from Baja to the United States, you must meet the following requirements:

- The dog must be at least six months old.
- The dog must have a microchip that can be scanned with a universal scanner.
- The dog must appear healthy upon arrival.
- The dog must have a current rabies vaccination certificate.
- The dog must have a receipt for a CDC Dog Import Form.
- The dog must have originated in a country with a low risk of rabies, such as Mexico or the U.S.

For whatever reasons, there are significantly fewer restrictions on cats. While the U.S. CDC recommends rabies vaccinations, proof of one is not required. Like dogs, however, cats are still subject to a physical inspection upon entry and can be denied entry if there is evidence of infection with a disease of public health concern.

Find official requirements from the U.S. government at this link: aphis. usda.gov

Veterinary Care in Baja

There is no shortage of veterinarians in Baja, but in most cases, vet care is different than in the U.S. How different will depend on the vet you see. Different is not necessarily a bad thing. In many instances, it's a positive, but sometimes, it can be a negative.

In my time in Baja, I owned two dogs that were failed by multiple vets. The worst offender was a sophisticated, large Ensenada clinic that closely resembled a U.S. vet's office. Do not let the trappings fool you; they do not necessarily indicate quality. Conversely, the smaller vets, who were extremely loving and caring, lacked the diagnostic equipment and facilities to help these dogs.

So, in my personal experience, the veterinary care in Baja has been great for simple, easily diagnosed conditions. But for serious issues, it can be tricky. I am sure there are vets equipped to handle cancer or other difficult-to-diagnose problems, but unfortunately, I did not find them near Ensenada in time.

How Veterinary Care in Baja is Different Than the US

- It's far more affordable! A vet visit in Baja should not fill you with financial dread as it does in the U.S. as it is highly affordable for routine care. Yes, it can get expensive if something is seriously wrong, but it is still more affordable than in the U.S.

- Most small vet offices lack the diagnostic facilities of U.S. vets, so you may be sent elsewhere for things like X-rays and lab work. They may or may not have an ultrasound machine.

- It's not unusual to find vets who make house calls for simple exams, vaccines, etc. This is especially useful if you have a pet that needs euthanizing.

- If you live in rural regions, farm vets can be terrific, especially for flea and tick medications, antibiotics, and simple issues. Our local farm vet, whose "office" is inside a feed store, also helped on a tragic weekend morning when my rescued cattle dog, howling in pain from cancer, needed to be euthanized as soon as possible.

Chapter 8: Housing in Baja

When it comes to housing in Baja, you will find many options at all points in the budget and amenities spectrums. You can rent, buy, or build, on or off the grid. RVers can live here full time too, or use the RV until they find their perfect home.

Before digging into this chapter, be sure to go back and read the sidebar on "camps" in Chapter 2, as this is a term you will come across a lot and it's important to understand what is meant by a "camp" in Baja because it is not necessarily the same as in the U.S.

Renting

Rents in Baja are significantly less than in the U.S., even in highly desirable, expensive areas like the beachfront or golf course resorts. Depending on the location, and the particular house, condo, or apartment, and the amenities offered, expect to pay in the neighborhood of $1200 - $2500 a month (U.S.) for a house on or very near the beach or golf course. If you live in town or in Mexican (as opposed to expat) neighborhoods and don't need anything fancy, rents can be shockingly low. A decent house for $300 or $400 a month (U.S.) is not out of the question.

Know that whatever rent you do end up paying, it's likely to remain at that rate even beyond the lease period. Generally speaking, landlords in Baja do not tend to raise the rent as regularly as they do in the U.S. If you are a good tenant who does not cause trouble and pays the rent every month, landlords are apt to leave rent rates alone for a long time, even if the rent you currently pay is under market value.

I recently spoke to former neighbors who just renewed their one-year lease for the ninth time. Despite signing a new lease each year, their rent has never been raised since they first moved in, even though rents in their beachside community have increased by about a quarter or more during that period.

I've had similar experiences myself as have many other friends and acquaintances. I know of a couple of friends right now who were considering moving to another beach area north of Ensenada, but the $900 a month rent they currently pay for their three-bedroom beachfront home south of Ensenada can no longer be found in today's market, so they are opting to stay put.

How Renting in Baja is Different

- I am sure there are exceptions, but landlords in Baja tend to be laxer than in the U.S. In addition to not regularly raising rents, they do not seem as concerned about it being right on time (contrast that with my Long Beach, CA landlord who after my being a tenant for over five years charged a late fee the one and only time the rent was one-day late because of an obvious bank error). My Baja neighbors and I had to regularly track down one Baja landlord to give him the rent each month as he was rarely in the office. Another had not noticed that we had moved out of a house for two months, despite giving a month's notice in advance.

- Again, not always, but usually, landlords are OK with you painting or making other changes (at your expense), as long as your changes do not negatively impact the value of the property.

- Yes, you will have a lease, but they are not as iron-clad as they are in the U.S. because enforcing leases in Mexico is both difficult and costly. Leases are more like a good idea under the best of circumstances. In most cases, there will be no repercussions if you break your lease. Of course, this works in both directions.

- Generally speaking, rental properties are not that well maintained in Baja, even in higher-end neighborhoods, so expect lots of little defects.

- Maintenance and repairs on rentals are usually not great in the U.S., but it's worse in Baja, and in many cases, it's just quicker and easier to fix simple things yourself.

- The rental deposits on the three rental houses I have leased during my time in Baja have each been the equivalent of one month's rent, meaning you will need two months' rent to move in. While it may vary from landlord to landlord, this is common.

- Credit and background checks rarely happen. If you have the deposit and the rent, that's enough for most landlords. Some might ask for a local reference. If you don't have one but you do have the money, you will probably get the rental anyway, especially if you offer a larger deposit.

- When I moved to Baja, a lot of people told me that ALL houses come furnished so I should get rid of my furniture. I find that is only sometimes true. Many rental houses are furnished. Sometimes even houses for sale come furnished. I suspect this is because when people move back to the States, it's easiest to leave it behind. But just as many places are not furnished. Either way, I don't recommend transporting a bunch of furniture to Baja, I talk more about why and what to do instead in Chapter 10.

- Rentals may or may not have appliances like refrigerators and washers and dryers. Even if they do, they may not be in the greatest condition. I talk about where to find deals on these in Chapter 11.

- Before signing a lease, verify who pays utilities and how, meaning do they stay in the landlord's name, which is easier and a common practice, or do you need to get them in your name? While getting the utilities in your name is a bit more of a hassle, it has benefits when it comes to residency visas as the government will accept utility bills (and little else) as proof of your legally living in the country. Learn more about temporary and permanent residency visas in Chapter 5.

- Verify how you get water and who pays for it. Water service in Baja is significantly different than in the U.S. or Canada, something I talk about in more detail in Chapter 11.

How to Avoid Rental and Real Estate Scams

Unfortunately, rental scams happen in Baja. If you rent from a credible landlord/camp (see Chapter 2) with a good reputation, or are in a large planned community or resort, you should be safe. Should, but not always.

The most common way both renters and buyers are scammed is by entering into a deal with a landlord or seller who does not actually own the property and who does not have the right to rent (or sell) it. As a side note, this happens in the U.S. too, as I learned when two young naïve college kids showed up at the door looking for the room they allegedly rented in my late sister's house. But it happens more frequently in Mexico. Scammers somehow get access to the property, take photos, and list it for sale or rent claiming it is theirs when it is not.

However, there are things you can and should always do to make sure you are not entering into a scam situation.

- Verify ownership, especially before buying but even when renting.
- I advise not to rent long term, and certainly never to buy, sight unseen. Besides being a common scammer tactic, you just can't tell from photos what a place is really like.

- If anyone is using hard sell tactics and pressuring you to give them money, for instance claiming several other tenants want the place so you had better jump on it, you should see it as a red flag and move on. Maybe it's legit, but it's usually not and likewise not worth the risk.

- When inspecting properties, make sure they match the description and that they are unoccupied, or if they are occupied talk to the current tenant to make sure they are indeed moving out.

- If something feels off, trust your instincts and walk away.

How to Find Long-Term Rentals in Baja

I cannot stress this strongly enough: you will find better housing options and deals once you are in Baja than you can find online before you go. This is why I always advise getting a short-term or month-to-month rental first, then look for your long-term home once you are there. Why?

- Many places are never listed online, so what you can find online is a far smaller inventory.

- It's difficult to get a true idea of what a place is like without seeing it in person. Online photos can be extremely deceiving.

- Some of these online offers are scams (see sidebar).

- Once you are there, you will meet people in the community. Let them know what you are looking for in a rental. This is a great way to get leads on places becoming available before they ever get listed. In some highly desirable beach areas, the search for housing in Baja is starting to resemble finding an apartment in New York City. In other words, being in town and ready to rent when someone moves or passes away (a lot of retirees live in Baja) can get you an amazing rental or even real estate deal that was never publicly listed.

Despite all of this, I constantly see Americans trying to conduct housing searches the same way they would at home. It just doesn't work that way here in most instances and is not the most effective method. Trust me: get a short term rental, go there, then find your dream home.

Alternatively, you can get the help of a credible relocation service or realtor. If you are dealing with a realtor, I highly recommend you get options and listings from several different agents as each one has their own, sometimes hidden, agendas.

When I was first starting to plan my move to Baja, I was introduced to a popular Punta Banda area real estate and rental agent at an Ensenada food festival event. She rather haughtily informed me that I needed to just forget about living on the beach because there was absolutely NOTHING available on the beach in Punta Banda. In reality, nothing could have been further from the truth. I happened across five different beach rentals in the first week of being there. They were not HER properties, but there were, in fact, plenty of beach rentals available. My friend and I ended up leasing one of them. Always verify or get a second opinion if you don't like what you are hearing.

When to Find Great Beach Rental Deals

You will usually luck into the best long term beach rental deals in late fall and winter. That's because the beaches of Baja are popular tourist destinations for both Mexican nationals and foreign visitors. Likewise, landlords can make more money on short-term vacation rentals, especially in the summer. But aside from holiday weeks, those short term renters become fewer and far between in the fall and winter. Lots of unoccupied rentals in the slow season can be the push some landlords need to make long term rental deals.

Owning Property in Baja

Unfortunately, even if you have the money, legally buying property in Baja is not quite as simple as in the U.S. That's because the Mexican Constitution prohibits direct ownership of real estate by foreigners in what is known as the "restricted zone" that encompasses all land located within 100 kilometers (about 62 miles) of any Mexican border, and 50 kilometers (about 31 miles) of any Mexican coastline. That encompasses most all of Baja.

While it is true that foreigners cannot hold property titles in their own names in the restricted zone, there are three ways for them to legally own a home and/or real estate in Baja:

- Through a bank trust.
- Through a corporation if the property is used for your business.
- By buying a house but leasing the land it sits upon.

Buying Land with a Bank Trust

According to my Mexican attorney, Carlos Victorica Reyes, a bank trust is absolutely the safest way for foreigners to own property in Baja, especially contrasted against the financial risks people regularly take by buying houses on leased land (more on this below).

Foreign individuals or companies, as well as Mexican companies that are 100% owned by foreigners, may purchase real estate for residential purposes within the restricted zone through a bank trust fund. The trust remains valid for 50 years and it can be renewed. The bank will retain the property title, but the foreigner is the beneficiary and may use the premises, may sell it, or will it to their heirs.

While this process might sound complicated and daunting, with the help of a good attorney, it's not.

Carlos says the reason this method of land ownership is so safe is because there are inspections and engineers involved, and most importantly, everything is notarized. He went on to explain that official notarized documents in Mexico carry a tremendous amount of legal weight. Unlike in the U.S., where notaries simply confirm signatories' identities, in Mexico they do far more, including preparing legal documents. Furthermore, becoming a notary in Mexico is a difficult and arduous process, but it results in an extremely lucrative career. Likewise, Carlos says no notary is going to risk their license and livelihood on a shady real estate deal.

A house bought in Baja through a bank trust, providing it meets the minimum government value requirement (see Chapter 5), can be counted as an asset when applying for permanent residence. If you intend to buy in Mexico, this is another way you can qualify. Another perk of permanent residency is that you will not have to pay capital gains taxes if you ever sell the property.

Carlos says you will see ads from attorneys in Baja promising a quick turnaround of two months or less on bank trusts, but he also warns consumers that this is unrealistic marketing hype. In most cases, anticipate the process of buying a house through a bank trust to take between three and a half to six months.

When it comes to cost, expect everything - including notaries, engineers, surveyors, inspectors, and attorneys - to be about 5% of the transaction total, not counting taxes.

Buying Land Through Forming a Mexican Corporation

Another way for foreigners to own land is by starting a Mexican corporation, as the corporation becomes the entity that holds the land title. If you are planning on starting a business in Mexico, this might be a good option for you. However, Carlos stresses that the property you buy MUST be used to run the business. In other words, you cannot start a corporation for the sole purpose of buying a residence. If you do, he says you will run into serious tax problems with the Mexican equivalent of the IRS. However, if the property is essential to the business, this is a viable and legal option.

A good example is my friend Sitara Monica Perez, founder of Valle Girl Vino in the Valle de Guadalupe. Sitara and her daughter formed a legal corporation for their businesses. The property they bought through that corporation is essential for their winery as there are vineyards as well as their ranch and tasting room, El Corcho Rosa (the Pink Cork). It also happens to be the site of their home, but the home is not the property's primary purpose.

Sitara says getting her business set up in Baja was not too difficult or expensive, except for the *Uso de Suelo* or land use permit, which was lengthy and costly. As she had a bilingual legal representative helping, she said it was pretty painless. In fact, the process of buying the property and starting the Mexican corporation was far less painful than keeping her small boutique winery running is. Between taxes, social security for her Mexican employees, licenses, inspections, and more, Sitara says she is constantly paying out. Not so different from running a business in the U.S.

Buying a Home on Leased Land

Buying a home on leased land in Baja is the least secure option. Despite it being filled with financial risks, it is an extremely common practice in Baja.

Even though it can be risky, in most cases it works out well. Expat Kristina Gandy had this to say about the experience she and her husband David had buying a house on leased land in Punta Banda's La Jolla Beach Camp, a place with a sterling reputation in the area:

"We got lucky finding an affordable house. We feel very safe in our neighborhood, and our landlord has a great reputation for being honest and fair. Not having to worry about water, security, and trash is one of the reasons why we decided to go with the land lease. Plus, our lease for an entire year is less than what we paid on our monthly mortgage for our house in Salt Lake City, Utah. We wouldn't change a thing."

While Kristina and David are happy, as are most residents in the La Jolla Beach Camp, it doesn't always work out that way. However, in every instance I have heard of someone getting majorly ripped off, the victim neglected to do their due diligence or opted to trust someone that the entire community had warned them not to. (Yes, community matters here, more on this in Chapter 12.)

There is an axiom of popular wisdom that regularly circulates among Baja expats on the topic of buying houses on leased land: "Never invest what you can't afford to lose." Meaning it is always a gamble.

It is essential you research before you buy, and I am talking deep research. You need to know that the person renting the land has the legal right to do so (see sidebar about avoiding scams), and that you are renting from a landlord you can trust not to change the agreement after the fact.

During my time in Baja, I have seen a number of naïve expats get into ridiculously bad deals -- deals they never in a million years would have even considered back home. An example is a former neighbor who, on nothing more than a handshake agreement, invested over $100K in renovating a large beach house. Supposedly he would be allowed to live out the rest of his days in the house rent-free, then it would then go back to the landlord in far better condition than when it started.

It seemed like a good bargain for both parties as the man was in his late 60s or early 70s, and the house had previously been completely uninhabitable. It did work out fine for about two years until the landlord, who did not have a good reputation in the community, decided that was enough free rent and gave my former neighbor the option to either start paying or move out.

While it was unfair, who in their right mind invests over $100K on a handshake deal, let alone with someone known to have questionable ethics at best? I suspect that copious amounts of tequila might have been involved.

Even in places with sterling reputations, if the patriarch or matriarch of the family passes, the children can and sometimes do fight, which can lead to land disputes. Likewise, there is always some risk in buying a house on leased land.

All that said, there are also some advantages to the practice, if you do your due diligence, have a good lease and contract, and minimize your risk.

Pros of Buying a Home on Leased Land in Baja:

- Buying a home on leased land is usually far more affordable than purchasing a property with full land ownership, especially in prime locations where land prices can be high. In addition to the reduced purchase price, there are lower upfront costs than buying property through a bank trust.

- Another advantage is flexibility. The lease can provide a fixed-term contract, giving homeowners the option to walk away from the property or sell the house at the end of the lease period without the complications involved in transferring land ownership. This might appeal to people who are unsure about their long-term plans or those looking to enjoy a property for a set period of time without the full commitment of owning land.

- The process of buying a home on leased land is quick, unlike buying property through a bank trust which usually takes between three and six months. If you have the money, you can buy a house on leased land and move into it right away.

- Land leases typically run for terms of five to ten years before needing to be renewed, so you will know your fixed costs.

Cons of Buying a Home on Leased Land in Baja:

- Uncertainty. Since the land is leased rather than owned, buyers do not have full control over the property in the long term. Once the lease expires, the landowner has the right to either renew the lease or take back the property, which could create uncertainty for homeowners. The terms of the lease may also increase over time, which can lead to higher costs for the homeowner as the lease renews.

- Securing financing for a home on leased land can be more challenging than for traditional properties and in most cases, it is out of the question, at least by traditional means (more below).

- While you can sell the house you buy, you will need the landlord's approval for the new buyer, and the lease may or may not stay the same.

How Buying a House on Leased Land Typically Works

Buying a house on leased land in Baja is nothing like any real estate deal you've ever had at home. In many ways, I would liken the experience more closely to buying a used car, albeit an expensive used car, than buying a house. It's far more casual than buying a house in the States or Canada. There are no official requirements as in most real estate deals. It is just an agreement between a buyer and a seller with the blessing of the landowner.

Coupled with the possible financial risks, the casual nature of these home-buying differences is likely to scare many expats off. That's OK. As we have discussed there is risk involved. Nonetheless, this is how things are regularly done in Baja.

Here are things to be aware of when contemplating buying a house on leased land:

- Because traditional financing for these houses is nearly impossible to obtain, these are often cash deals. You pay the owner, usually through an escrow account (recommended), and then he or she signs over the house to you, based upon the landowner's approval.

- Because it is a basic deal between buyer and seller, a realtor may or may not be involved. Just like in the U.S. some realtors in Baja are great, others not so much. For instance, because of his own hidden agenda, the realtor representing a house my friend and I wanted to purchase on leased land in La Bufadora blew up the deal we had already negotiated with the owner.

- The terms are often negotiable. After all, not everyone has enough cash on hand to buy a house outright, even a house that is inexpensive by U.S. or Canadian standards. Likewise, rather than wait around for somebody who does have enough cash, some sellers might be willing to take payments or enter into a lease-to-own situation. It never hurts to inquire.

- If you do have all cash, you can sometimes negotiate a lower price, something you usually won't be able to do when making payments.

- While home inspections are not required, I would definitely advise you to get one before buying any property. Homes in Baja are notoriously under-maintained and you need to know if you will be taking on any major repair bills before buying a house. Such repairs may or may not be a deal breaker for you, but they can be a negotiating point to get a lower price, and it's important to count any essential repairs into your budget.

- The reputation of the landowner matters! Do your research and ask around in the community. Don't just research online where people are less apt to be honest about negative experiences with locals (more on this in Chapter 12). Instead, privately take some locals who know the landlord out for happy hour or invite them over for dinner and get them talking. You'll learn far more.

The bottom line is, buying a home on leased land in Baja can be a good option for some buyers who are willing to accept the limitations and uncertainties of leasehold ownership. It's important to carefully review the lease terms, understand the risks, and weigh the benefits of lower initial costs against the potential for higher long-term costs or complications when it comes time to sell or renew the lease.

Building, Modular Homes, and Manufactured Homes

You will notice a lot of modular, prefab, and manufactured homes throughout Baja. Those into sustainable architecture will especially enjoy drives through the Valle de Guadalupe, where you will find lots of creative and artistic examples, both in the homes, and the hotels, resorts, and wineries.

Movable homes, such as manufactured (mobile) homes and container homes, make a lot of sense in Baja for several reasons:

- The fact that you can move them makes the having a home on leased land scenario that we talked about above, less risky. Yes, moving a manufactured or modular home involves work and expense. It's not something you would want to do often. Nonetheless, the fact that you can take your home with you should you want or need to move, should provide some financial peace of mind.

- Northern Baja has a decent infrastructure for these types of dwellings, so you will be able to find sales and support, as well as movers. In fact, most of the places where you can buy manufactured homes will include delivery and setup in the cost.

- Zoning restrictions on where you can put manufactured homes are far looser than in the U.S., and in many areas, nonexistent.

- Because so many bricks and sticks houses are under-maintained, buying a new modular or manufactured home lets you know you are moving into a house that's in good condition. This is especially important in beach areas where, because of the constant moisture and lack of proper insulation and maintenance, a lot of houses develop mold issues.

When it comes to building a new home in Baja, old timers who have not been there in decades will tell you that it's the "wild, wild west," meaning there are no laws or permits like in the U.S. when it comes to construction and real estate. NOT TRUE! Maybe it used to be that way, but it hasn't been for a long time.

There are, in fact, many laws and rules and a lot of red tape. It's true those rules and laws are often different than in the U.S., but they do exist. Some things may be easier, but others will be more difficult.

For instance, a workshop I attended a few years ago in the U.S. about building with hempcrete was filled with students planning on building in Mexico because they would have an easier time getting permitted for this relatively unknown building material in Mexico than at home.

However, hearing horror stories from others who have built, navigating the cultural differences and the laws and red tape can be extremely daunting. Add that to the fact that construction projects, which are never simple or easy under the best of circumstances, are always more difficult if you are not fluent in the local language. I am not saying it can't be successfully done, but a good attorney and a good contractor are essential.

RVing in Baja — Traveling or Stationary

If you have an RV, consider bringing it to Baja. It can provide a residence while you look for a full time home. If you are comfortable living in your RV, it can even be your full-time home as many camps will lease long-term RV lots. As recreational vehicles are so easy to move, should you want or need, this scenario takes away the risk of living on leased land, should you find such a space.

When it comes to RV campgrounds, both coasts of Baja offer LOTS of options at all ends of the price and amenity spectrum, from gated luxury RV resorts to basic Mom and Pop coastal fish camps that allow dispersed, self-contained, off-grid camping on their properties. And everything in between.

Check in advance on services and how you access them, especially if you intend to RV into more remote areas. For instance, the electrical hookup you get might mean plugging into the wall outlet in the nearby bathroom, as opposed to having a 30 or 50-amp tower next to your rig like you would at a U.S. campground. Water may or may not be included, but you can always get it. You will always want to carry drinking water, as well. Learn more about water in Baja in Chapter 11.

Prices for campgrounds can vary greatly depending on where you go and who you know. Some of the expat-dominated high-end resort campgrounds are starting to mirror U.S. rates. Well, maybe not quite, but they aren't cheap either.

Conversely, deals can be had, and it will be easier to find them once you are there and can ask around, just as it is when you are looking for regular housing.

For instance, my beachside RV space winter rental south of Ensenada is at a camp that has some RV spaces, but mostly vacation rentals and full-time homes. They do not market themselves as an RV park, but I had gotten to know the landlord when I had previously rented a house there. For two winters in a row, he rented me a full hookup space for a mere $300 a month (in 2022 and 2023). Was it like a U.S. campground? Not at all. My electricity came from an extension cord plugged into the empty house next door that the camp uses for maintenance and storage. The water came from a *pila* (more on water in Baja in Chapter 11), so I was always using my RV's pump for plumbing, showers, and dishes, but I had plenty of water. There were no public showers or bathrooms.

On the other hand, I was living in a safe and secure gated camp with an ocean view for $300 a month. I could literally be at the water's edge in seconds and the sound of the waves lulled me to sleep each night. Not bad tradeoffs!

Is Baja Big Rig Friendly?

It depends. You will have no trouble driving a big motorhome or towing a large 5th wheel or trailer in the areas we are discussing in this book. In other words, between the border and Ensenada on the west side of the peninsula or between the border and San Felipe on the east side. The toll roads are well maintained, and you will also find a fair amount of choices for big rig friendly campgrounds.

South of those points, it gets sketchier. Roads are not as well maintained and they get windy, narrow, and lack shoulders. Services and amenities get sparse too.

There's a reason Baja is a van lifer's paradise. Generally, the smaller the RV the better for travel. It's not that it's not possible in bigger rigs, but it would definitely be stressful. If you are planning to travel and then park in one spot for a long while, it might be worth it.

Vintage RV Treasures

One more note for those who love vintage RVs. Some of the homes for sale or lease have been built around vintage RVs and mobile homes, as many beach properties started as vacation camps and have morphed into permanent homes through the decades. This can be very cool if you are into such things (or the height of tackiness if you are not).

If you like restoring old RVs, there are treasures in various states of disrepair to be found all over Baja. In the old days, people would go to Baja, set up camps, and never bother to move those RVs out when they moved back to the States. In other cases, the owners passed away and their families had no interest in Great Grandpa's old Airstream or Spartan left behind in Mexico, even if it was an otherwise highly collectible and valuable vintage relic. These trailers sit abandoned, waiting for someone to make the landowner an offer and come and rescue and restore them.

Chapter 9: *Dinero* (Money)

Money makes the world go around and, as Baja is part of the world, there are financial considerations you must take into account when making such a move. However, Baja's proximity to the U.S. makes many of these issues easier to deal with than they would be in a more distant locale.

For instance, as most banking is done online these days, many expats never bother to get a Mexican bank account. It's easy to get cash whenever needed from ATMs. Of course, this will depend on your personal circumstances. If you must pay household and utility bills, or if you work or run a business in Mexico, a Mexican bank account will be necessary. On the other hand, if you rent and the landlord pays the utilities, you might not need it.

Expats and the U.S. IRS

Know that because of the U.S.'s Foreign Account Tax Compliance Act (FATCA), foreign banks are required to report U.S. citizens' local accounts to the IRS, so there is no hiding your Mexican bank account from Uncle Sam.

Even without a Mexican bank account, and contrary to popular belief, filing and paying taxes to your host country does not mean that you're off the hook with the U.S. This is true in Mexico or in any other country you might choose to live. The United States and the tiny East African country of Eritrea are the only two countries in the entire world still holding onto citizenship-based taxation!

This rule applies even if:

- You hold dual citizenship.
- You've been an immigrant who has lived in another country for 50 years or more.
- You are a citizen by birth who has never lived in the United States, for instance, if your parents left shortly after you were born.

There are some exceptions. U.S. tax law does allow some expat taxpayers to take a foreign income exclusion, but know that this only reduces your regular income tax, it does nothing for your self-employment tax.

Of course, these rules apply to people earning their incomes in Mexico. Find details here: irs.gov

Check with your accountant for details about your specific circumstances and tax liabilities. For retirees and people not working in Mexico, little should change concerning your U.S. taxes, but you still need to file them.

Cash is King

When I am in the U.S. I rarely carry much cash. Almost everywhere takes credit cards, I get airline miles by using them, and it helps keep my expenses easy to account for and categorize come tax time. However, Mexico runs on cash and MANY places do not accept credit cards. You will need to carry more cash in Baja. Also, you will always want to keep change on hand for tips (learn more about tipping in Chapter 12).

Of course, in tourist areas, most shops and restaurants will take credit cards. Outside of that, they may or may not. If it is a higher-end restaurant, you have a 50/50 shot, but even many of these are cash only. Supermarkets take cards, but the small bodegas and shops essential to village life in Baja usually do not.

You can't even always count on the gas stations either. If the internet is out, which happens more frequently in Baja than in the States, you will be out of luck. Some remote places do not accept cards at all. For instance, when I visited friends on Gonzaga Bay, a few hours south of San Felipe, the only gas station for MANY miles only accepted cash.

Pay Attention to Currency Exchange Rates and ATM Fees

It's easy to obtain cash in Baja from currency exchange shops or ATM machines. However, the rates of exchange can and do change. Savvy expats will do themselves a favor and pay attention to these fluctuations, as when you draw cash out of your American bank account can affect your bottom line.

For instance, in 2024 the dollar-to-peso value dipped as low as $16.26 pesos to the dollar in April and rose to as high as $20.71 in November. Four and a half pesos as change in your pocket is not much money, but when you are exchanging hundreds of dollars in currency it adds up quickly. Pay attention to exchange rates and predictions. Whenever possible, exchange money or draw out cash from your U.S. account(s) when rates are favorable.

Speaking of drawing cash, the downside of getting cash from an ATM is that, just like in the U.S., fees are involved. It pays to shop around as different banks' ATMs have different fees. The machine will always let you know the exchange rate and fees before completing the transaction, so you can always cancel it should you choose.

Some bank cards will refund those ATM fees, so it also pays to shop around for the accounts you use to draw cash from. Charles Schwab is one example; however, their exchange rates are often not as favorable as others, so it may or may not be a savings in the end.

Working in Baja

A lot of people moving to Baja are retirees for whom work is no longer an issue. But many still need to make a living, whether it is a full time living or a supplemental income to social security or pensions.

There are several income generating options available to expats, however, the most unrealistic one, yet the one I hear potential expats talk most about, is getting a job in Baja. For all practical purposes, let's take that one off the table, unless you are an expert in some highly sought-after field that causes Mexican corporations to fight over you. Not only will you raise the ire of Mexican natives if you take a job away from a citizen, in most cases the job will not pay well enough for you to want it in the first place.

I am not saying that well-paying jobs in Baja don't exist, but they are not the norm. Furthermore, all jobs in Mexico pay far, far less than in the U.S. and Canada. To give you an idea, Mexico just raised their daily minimum wage to 278.88 pesos (about $13.75 U.S. dollars as of this writing). Even in the Northern Border Zone, including Baja, where wages are higher by law, the new daily minimum wage for 2025 is only $419.88 pesos ($20.65 dollars per day or barely over $100 per week/$400 per month).

Realistic Ways of Making Money While Living in Baja

What's an expat who needs to make a living to do? You do have options:

Working Remotely: Many remote workers who can do their jobs or run their businesses from anywhere with an internet connection, call Baja home. This is a viable employment option as there are so many possible online jobs. One word of caution: plan for connectivity redundancy. It's not that internet connections are unstable in Baja, but they do go out more frequently than in the U.S. It's never for long, but any interruption when you need to work can be maddening, and can possibly jeopardize your job. The remote workers I know usually get two providers, just to be safe. Or they have a Starlink dish, as the satellite internet service is extremely reliable everywhere, even when other services are out.

Seasonal Work: I know of other expats who work seasonally. They will go to the States for several months, complete their seasonal jobs, and then go back home to Baja until the following season.

Starting a Business in Mexico: If your legal residency is in order, it's not that difficult to start a business in Mexico. You will need an accountant who will help you set up the business entity and make quarterly tax payments. My Canadian expat neighbor Thomas Rogan, a man who always does everything meticulously by the book, was amazed at how simple it was to start his mobile sound business. Furthermore, if your business needs a physical location, you can form a Mexican corporation, which is one way that foreigners can own property in Baja. I talk more about this in Chapter 8.

Working in the U.S. and Living in Baja: This is a viable option for both expats and Mexican nationals who work in San Diego and commute to Tijuana or Rosarito. Make no mistake about it, border crossings can be a time-sucking hassle. I would not want to do this every workday. But thousands of people do. This option might make more sense for those with short work weeks. Some of these folks also have places to stay north of the border during the work week, then they go back to Baja on the off days.

Part III
Living Life in Baja

If you've made it this far in the book, you have probably decided to make the move to Baja. This section covers the move itself, and setting up your new home south of the border, along with local customs and culture that may be new to you.

Chapter 10: The Move Itself

OK. You've done your research. You've checked it out. You've decided to move. It's now time to get you and your stuff to Baja. For most people, the first order of business will be to downsize. Yes, you can move all your household belongings to Mexico, but most people don't because the cost of moving them versus buying household items in Mexico often doesn't make sense. Plus, you may not have a place to put all that stuff right away, not to mention the house you buy or rent might come furnished. You will have to weigh these factors for yourself and your circumstances and decide what makes the most sense for you.

Downsizing can be a stumbling block that keeps many people from ever accomplishing their goals of leaving the country. I will go into strategies of what to take and leave behind below, but generally speaking, the more you downsize and the less you need to move to Mexico, the better.

When my friend and I moved, we were living in a huge four-bedroom house with an even bigger four-car garage. While we weren't hoarders, the stuff we had managed to accumulate through the decades had nonetheless become overwhelming. We had so much stuff that our stuff owned us, and it created a low-grade depression that was with us all the time.

Once the job was over, we found downsizing tremendously liberating. That low-grade depression disappeared with all our junk and we instantly felt lighter. However, getting to that point was not easy.

The task of downsizing all our stuff was so daunting that we kept procrastinating on it. Finally, I came to the conclusion that if I did not come up with a solid plan, accompanied by hard deadlines, it was never going to get done, and we would consequently never move.

How to Downsize Before Moving to Baja

My friend and I did accomplish this gargantuan task, and you can too. Start by getting out your calendar and making a plan. Yes, write it down either on paper or online. Hold yourself accountable by giving yourself a firm yet realistic deadline by which you want to be in a position to pack up your remaining possessions and move them to Mexico.

Wait, there's more. You will also want to give yourself deadlines within that bigger deadline for accomplishing each of the tasks below. (As a side note, if money is not an issue and you don't care about selling your stuff, or if you don't have anything of value to sell, skip ahead to Step #4.)

#1. Go through your entire home, inside and out, including the garage, attic, and basement, and start by separating out anything of high value. For this first sweep, I am talking about things that might need to go to an auction house or that might take time to find the right buyer with the right resources. For instance, valuable art, jewelry, rare coins, or collectibles. If you have these types of things, get them listed wherever you will sell them.

#2. If you need to sell any extra vehicles, boats, RVs, snowmobiles, jet skis, ATVs, etc., get those large items listed for sale and move those tasks off your plate, although the watercraft and ATVs you might want to consider bringing to Baja.

#3. Next, go through the entire house again and separate out anything you can sell yourself, for instance by listing on eBay, Next Door, or Facebook Marketplace. Get those listings up and move that stuff out.

#4. Now, go through the house, garage, basement, and attic again, but focus on only one room at a time. Don't forget to also deal with possessions that live outside, like patio furniture, grills, etc. Do not move on to a new room or area until you have completed the downsizing process for the room you are working on. Give yourself a deadline for sorting through each room or area. Separate things into these piles:

- Things you want to keep. I urge you to be brutal about how much you keep. If it is not essential or highly sentimental, get rid of it. See sidebar for tips.

- If you intend to have an estate sale/moving sale/garage sale, start a place to put all those items. Put the date of the sale on your calendar so you have a deadline for that too.

- Things to be donated to a thrift store or listed for free online.

- Move things destined for the trash directly into the dumpster.

#5. Once you have sorted through your home, move out the thrift store and free piles.

#6. Have your moving sale.

#7. After all this, you will probably still have furniture and a bunch of miscellaneous items that didn't sell to get rid of. We had a BBQ, invited a bunch of friends over, and let them take anything they wanted, right down to things like an abundance of spices and condiments in the kitchen that we were not going to move. Friends were also welcome to help themselves to anything at our moving sale, which took place the day before, and of course from the thrift store and free piles along the way.

#8. If after this, you still have furniture and big items you don't want to have to move yourself, listing them for sale for a very low price or even for free on the Next Door app or Facebook Marketplace will result in your neighbors doing the heavy lifting work of moving them out for you.

That's essentially it. Pack up the remainder of your belongings and you should be ready to move to Baja!

Beware of Perceived Value Objects When Downsizing

People who have not done a lot of market research tend to overestimate their stuff's value. Sometimes someone has inaccurately estimated an object's value to them; sometimes, a relative told them about the value of a "family heirloom;" sometimes it is all in their heads.

As someone who has dabbled in selling art, antiques, and collectibles for decades, I have observed this common layperson's error a lot. However, indulging in this behavior can seriously hold up your downsizing project and in some cases, keep you from ever moving. Don't make these mistakes. Here are four real-life examples:

- My friend had a painting from his late uncle, a known artist who was exhibited in galleries and museums. My friend thought this was something he had to hold on to even though he didn't aesthetically like the art. He informed me that the painting "was his retirement." A quick perusal of an art website told me at most the painting, a small study, was worth about $1500. However, nothing could convince my friend that the painting wasn't worth a fortune. He died with it tucked away in a back closet when it was then passed on to another relative who now proudly displays it.

- Another friend worked at Mattel in the old days and had a rare prototype Hot Wheels car he was convinced was worth hundreds of thousands of dollars. Even if that were true - and it's not - finding a buyer that will fork over that much cash isn't easy, and you certainly aren't likely to find them without the help of a serious auction house. I am not saying that this collectible doesn't have value, it does, but it's nowhere near what my friend thinks it is. He probably could still use the help of a good auction house, but as far as I know, the collectible toy remains packed away in a random box in his Southern California garage.

- A distant relative was convinced her collection of "rare" Beanie Babies was worth tens of thousands of dollars. Maybe some of those toys were fetching big bucks at the moment when that fad was at its zenith, but guess what? Nobody cares anymore, and her collection is now virtually worthless.

- Here's a value mistake I made myself. For years I thought that the things that were valuable antiques when I was a child, like my mother and grandmother's cut glass crystal and formal tableware and dishes, were still valuable. Styles change. Lifestyles change. Nobody wants that stuff anymore. While I know my mother was spinning in her grave, we literally could not give some of these items away for free at our moving sale.

Be careful of getting caught in a trap of putting off downsizing or moving until you get what you think things are worth. You may not ever get it, but meanwhile, your life will march on. Before you know it, like my friend with the painting in his closet, it will be too late. When downsizing, the primary purpose is not to make money. It's great when you can, but don't let making money make you lose focus from your primary goal of downsizing to move.

How to Let Go: Dealing with Sentimental Objects when Downsizing

When it comes to family heirlooms and sentimental objects that mean a lot to you, find a way to keep them IF they truly mean a lot to you. However, I urge you to downsize these where and when you can. For instance, photos and videos can be digitized. Doing this task alone cut several LARGE moving boxes for me.

Also, ask yourself if the feelings are genuine, and if they are, does that sentimentality belong to you or someone else? For example, I carried my late mother and aunt's crystal and formal dishes around for decades, despite it not being my style and not being anything I ever used. (Side note: Does anyone use sterling flatware anymore? Nope. But selling it for the price of silver to be melted down netted me several thousand dollars.)

It took moving to another country for me to admit to myself that I was only keeping these things because of who they once belonged to. These objects really meant nothing to me personally, and they had nothing to do with my love for my late family. Once I came to terms with that and separated the emotion from the objects, I was able to let them go. Ultimately, downsizing these items made me feel substantially freer, and doing so definitely made my move to Baja far easier.

When it comes to things you think you must keep, follow organizing expert Marie Kondo's advice and ask yourself if the object brings you joy. Also, ask yourself if you would miss the thing's presence in your day-to-day life. If you answered yes, then find a way to keep it. If not, bless it and let it go!

Another way of getting rid of things with sentimental (or real) value that are not practical to keep or move is by gifting them to family and friends (assuming said family and friends want the objects in question). I did this a lot when I moved. Now, whenever I visit, I am surrounded by familiar furniture, art, and objects that my loved ones are enjoying. That makes me happy.

What To Take, What to Leave Behind

These suggestions assume that your goal is to move as little as possible to Baja. However, if you are hiring a moving truck/service, you can take more. But even then, space is money, so you are going to want to pare things down.

Usually, when crossing the border, you are only allowed to bring in $300 US worth of goods without paying a duty. In my experience,

Mexican customs agents are extremely generous in determining the value of used goods, meaning they value used goods low. Likewise, you shouldn't have to pay exorbitant fees even when you do declare items.

However, according to the real estate site Baja 123, which helps expats relocate to Baja, there is a one-time exception to the $300 tax-free limit when you are moving to Mexico. This exemption allows you to bring new or used consumer goods necessary for your personal use into Mexico without paying fees. To do so, you MUST have your FMM card or temporary or permanent residence visa (see Chapter 5). You will prepare and present a list of the goods you are bringing to the consulate, then you will work with a customs agent to determine the value of your belongings and to help you apply for the permit. The permitting process takes 24 hours, so plan an extra day near the border when moving.

Some moving companies in Mexico are connected with customs agents and can help you move through this process, so if you are going to use a mover, you might want to seek one out that offers this service.

 Find more details at this link: baja123.com

What to Get Rid Of

- Most Furniture: Many homes in Mexico come furnished, and even in those that don't, your current furniture likely won't match the house. Unless it holds sentimental or collectible value and you love it, leave furniture behind. I talk about where to find deals on furnishings in Baja in Chapter 11.

- Media: Books, records, videos, etc. are now available digitally. Not moving media easily reduced our move by a dozen or more large boxes.

- Winter Sports Equipment and Clothing: You won't need them in Baja.

- Knickknacks and tchotchkes unless they have sentimental value.

- Seasonal items and decorations unless they hold sentimental value.
- Anything frivolous or unnecessary.

Beyond this, you can easily get anything and everything you need to set up a house once you are in Baja. If you don't mind second-hand, you can get it all very inexpensively. (More on this in Chapter 11.)

When in doubt, leave it behind. My friend and I never missed or needed a single thing we left behind, save our tall expandable ladder. We could have used that as two of the beach homes we lived in had tall, vaulted ceilings, stairways, and balconies.

What to Keep

- Things of important sentimental value that can't be replaced.
- Your favorite art pieces.
- Electronics, as these are more expensive in Mexico.
- Clothing and personal items.
- Summer and water sports equipment.
- Hobby and pastime tools and supplies, as these may be harder to find in Baja, depending on the hobby.
- I also brought kitchen supplies like cookware and small appliances, although you can also find all of these in Mexico. If you are a foodie you will want to bring your toys as they are part of your hobby.

Optional

- Large appliances: As electronics in Mexico tend to be more expensive, you might want to move these if you own quality high-end appliances like refrigerators, freezers, washers, or dryers. On the other hand, used appliances are plentiful and affordable in Baja.

- When it comes to dishes and glassware, it's a toss-up. If you are attached to them, bring them, otherwise leave them behind and start anew to match your new home and lifestyle.

- Tools. If you have expensive tools you use, bring them. Otherwise, you can easily and inexpensively find basic tools once you are there (more in Chapter 11).

Bring Your Coffee Grinder!

Coffee hounds take note! You will be hard-pressed to find coffee grinders in Baja. Whole bean coffee is also less prominent although you can find it at Costco, some supermarkets, and specialty roasters. But when my coffee grinder quit on me a while back, there was not a one to be found in the entire greater Ensenada area, not even at Costco or Walmart!

Moving Strategies: How to Get Your Stuff to Baja

No matter which moving plan you choose, you will have to find a way to get your things to the border or close to the border on the U.S. side. After that, there are three options for how to get your stuff the rest of the way to your new home in Baja, Mexico:

- Hire a moving company
- Hire an individual with a truck
- Do it yourself

A moving company that specializes in moving people across the border is going to make sense for a lot of people, especially those coming from long distances and those who have a lot to move. Not only are they used to the process, but many of these companies can help you streamline it and clear the necessary permits and paperwork (see above). An internet search for the area you want to move will bring up options, as will asking for recommendations in the local social media groups (see Chapter 12).

Another option when checking out the social media boards is to find an entrepreneurial individual with a truck or cargo trailer who will move your things from the U.S. side of the border to your new Baja digs. They probably won't help with the paperwork, but they should be familiar enough with the process to at least advise you. As with all services, invest some time vetting any local movers before hiring them.

Moving yourself to Mexico is another option, especially if you have sufficiently downsized to the point where you can pack everything in your vehicle(s). Or your vehicle and a cargo trailer.

If you can't quite fit everything in your vehicle in a single trip, another thought is to rent a storage unit just over the border on the U.S. side and then move everything down to Baja over several trips. This option worked for my friend and me. However, just as in planning for the move, give yourself a hard deadline to get everything moved out. Storage unit fees aren't cheap, and they keep accumulating month after month. The U-Haul storage facility close to the border that I used seems to consistently have a three-month move-in special running that gives you a free month. Make sure you get yourself completely moved out by the end of those three months.

One downside to the storage unit method of moving is that you cannot use the duty-free household moving exemption for each of those trips, only one. However, the good news is that customs officials tend to underestimate the value of used household goods.

Chapter 11: Setting Up House in Baja

Once you have arrived at your new Baja home it's time to set up house. If you opted for a short-term rental until you find your long term home, you might not need much of anything, as these are usually furnished, right down to the kitchenware. But if you have found a place you intend to settle into, you are likely going to need a lot of things.

Where to Find Deals on Any and All Household Goods

You will have no trouble finding new furniture and home goods in northern Baja's larger cities, such as Tijuana, Rosarito, and Ensenada. But if you don't mind shopping in second-hand stores, known as *segundas*, you can find anything and everything to outfit a home, right down to linens and cutlery.

The Mexican culture is far less disposable than the U.S., a very good thing in my opinion. Everything of any value is rescued and finds its way to a *segunda*. *Segunda* shopping is like treasure hunting. You never know what you'll find. Some days are busts, other days you'll find too much good stuff.

You'll find *segundas* all over Baja, sometimes alone, sometimes grouped together. For instance, Ensenada's *Los Globos* area spans multiple city blocks filled with nothing but *segunda* stores. Some are organized and easy to shop in, others you will have to dig. But you will find good stuff if you do. For instance, digging through some cutlery bins, I found several Le Creuset knives and kitchen accessories. I paid about .25 cents each for these treasures that I found mixed in with low-quality dollar-store kitchenware. I also found a set of collectible signed California pottery plates from the 60s, again mixed among common commercial dinnerware, for about $1 US per plate. These experiences illustrate how if you know brands and quality and are not afraid to look through *segunda* store piles, you will be amazed at what you can find. I have even found artwork that later sold at prestigious U.S. auction houses.

Much of the furniture at *segundas* is imported from the U.S. You can find some stylish, high-quality items for pennies on the dollar. And don't forget, getting things reupholstered in Baja is inexpensive, and shops doing this work are plentiful. If you find furniture with good bones but a worn exterior, buy it and give it a new life in your style and colors.

It was over eight years ago when I first moved. At that time, I bought furniture for a two-bedroom house, including living room, bedrooms (minus mattresses), and other miscellaneous tables and bookcases, for less than $400…delivered! Even my Mexican friends were astounded at how inexpensive it was.

Some *segundas* benefit charities, much like thrift stores in the States. Others are businesses that support the store owner's families. Many *segundas* specialize, which makes it easy when outfitting a home. One store will have washers and dryers, another furniture, another mattresses, another linens and textiles, etc.

In addition, a lot of the weekly farmer's markets in Baja also have areas where vendors sell new and used merchandise, so these also merit checking out.

Lastly, you can find lots of great deals on furniture and appliances on Facebook Marketplace. Just as in the States, there are scammers here, so vet purchases before handing over money. Nonetheless, there are many legitimate deals to be had.

Utilities

Depending on where you live, your landlord might pay the utilities. In some cases, utilities will be included with the rent, although more commonly the landlord will give you a monthly bill for your share of the utilities. In some rental cases, you can get the utilities in your name. Your landlord can advise you on how. This has advantages if you are trying to prove your residency in Mexico for immigration purposes (more in Chapter 5).

If you own the house through any of the scenarios we discussed in Chapter 8, you will need to contract with the utility company for your electricity. Usually. In some camps, such as the La Jolla Beach Camp south of Ensenada, homeowners pay the landowner a monthly electricity bill along with maintenance fees for trash collection and security, so the scenarios can vary.

If you do get the utilities in your name, you will need to pay a deposit, and it is easiest to have a Mexican bank account for this (see Chapter 9).

Besides electricity, most homes in Baja run on propane for things like the stove, the water heater, and the clothes dryer. Likewise, most homes are outfitted with a large propane tank outside. Check for details on propane when renting or buying. Delivery trucks are plentiful so keeping your propane tank filled is not an issue, and a single tank can last for months.

Some urban areas might have natural gas lines, which you will deal with the gas company for these bills.

Water

Water in Baja is substantially different than in the U.S. To begin with, unless you install an expensive, sophisticated filtration system in your home, you will never drink the water from the tap. Tap water is just for washing and cleaning.

How that tap water gets into your home might be different too. In some neighborhoods, especially in cities, the water might be plumbed in from a central source. Some camps and planned communities also offer this. But equally common is an individual large water tank that serves a single residence. Known as a *pila*, how long the water will last will depend on the size of your tank and your water usage habits, but it typically lasts a good while. For instance, with three people flushing toilets, showering, doing laundry, and dishes, without skimping, we never had to fill the *pila* more than once a month.

As everyone in your neighborhood will need water services, delivery trucks are always nearby and can usually be there within a half hour. In a lot of camps, you just need to call the office or the security gate and ask them to send the water truck over.

As EVERYONE also needs drinking water, bottled drinking water services are plentiful and extremely inexpensive in Baja. How inexpensive? I usually tip the guy who loads the heavy bottles in my car as much or more than the cost of the water. Many places also offer home delivery for a nominal fee. You can even readily find alkaline drinking water for a slightly higher price but still substantially less expensive than regular bottled drinking water in the States.

Phone

Navigating phone service, especially if you still have strong connections to the U.S., can be challenging. The easiest solution is to keep your U.S. number and also get a Mexican phone number. You don't necessarily need a second phone if your phone takes two SIM cards, and most do these days. Simply toggle between your two numbers as needed.

Some people might be able to get away with just keeping one number, but most will benefit from both:

- **U.S. Phone Number:** Many U.S. banks, government agencies, and online services require an American number for two-factor authentication or customer service calls. Ditto if you are Canadian. Even with an American number, these things can still be frustrating when you are calling from another country, but without it, you can forget about it. A U.S. or Canadian number will usually let you receive calls or texts from your contacts from home without fees, and it keeps access to apps and services that are linked to your home number intact.

- **Mexican Phone Number:** Having a Mexican phone number will make it easier to connect to local services. It will also save you on expensive roaming charges, and in theory, you will have better network connectivity in Baja with a Mexican provider.

Baja Runs on WhatsApp

In Baja, along with most of Latin America, having WhatsApp installed on your phone is essential. Far more than just a messaging app, it's the primary way people communicate here, both personally and professionally. You will need WhatsApp to coordinate with contractors, service providers, mechanics, handymen, housekeepers, and other businesses. Many small businesses even prefer WhatsApp for inquiries and quotes. If you interact socially with Mexicans, you will also find WhatsApp necessary when making plans and meeting up.

Internet

Internet service in Baja, while generally reliable, is less reliable than in most areas of the United States. Dropouts and service interruptions happen - not every day, and they usually don't last for more than a few hours - but they happen semi-regularly, especially during stormy weather. If you don't depend on the internet, it's frustrating, but if you do, it can be maddening. Most expats who depend on the internet for work get two providers so that one will always be working.

Another good option is Starlink satellite internet which works from any place with a clear view of the sky. Starlink is more expensive, although insider tip, it costs less if you buy it in Mexico than in the U.S. Having Starlink eliminates the need for local providers.

If you get the mobile version of Starlink, it can travel with you all over Baja (and the U.S. and Canada, too, for that matter), and you will always have fast, reliable internet service. Outside of the populated areas of Baja that we have talked about in this book, Starlink is the only way to stay connected, and it has dramatically changed the lives of people living off-grid in Baja's more remote regions.

Voting as an Expat

Voting while living in Mexico will depend on how you decide to handle mail delivery. If you plan to keep a U.S. address, you can get an absentee ballot sent there and vote by mail, at least in California as well as in many other states. This option will only be practical if you frequently visit where the U.S. mail is delivered.

Alternatively, you can vote from Mexico. U.S. citizens living in other countries can receive an absentee ballot by email, fax, or internet download, depending on the state they are eligible to vote in. Find more information from the State Department's website at state.gov

---

Getting Mail and Deliveries in Baja

There is no public home mail delivery in Baja, which is a huge difference from the US. Here's how expats in Northern Baja cope with this:

- Keep a U.S. mailbox near the American side of the border and pick up mail when you go north.

- Keep a U.S. mailbox and hire someone to bring you your mail. Entrepreneurial folks in expat communities all over Baja offer this weekly or bi-weekly service. You will usually have to have a box where the service picks up. For instance, many people in the community where I live have mailboxes at The Mail Room in Imperial Beach, California, just over the border, as a few different services in our area pick up there. The local Facebook group for the area where you want to live can help you find such a service.

- Get a private mailbox and address in Baja. Yes, private mailbox services exist in Baja. Get yourself one, and you have a Mexican address where you can receive mail.

- Amazon pick-up boxes are popping up in high-population areas of Baja. To use these, you must order from Amazon in Mexico. Some expats are even getting Amazon Mexico deliveries at their homes. I have heard mixed reviews on the success of this, but it seems to be improving, and I expect it to only get better over time.

Duties and Customs on Packages

If you get goods and packages at your U.S. mailbox, those are subject to duties when you cross the border into Mexico. The current exemption is $300, so if the value of the products you are bringing in exceeds that, you will need to enter the "something to declare" line when you cross from the U.S. into Mexico and let the customs agent know. This is not a big deal and shouldn't add a lot of time to your commute.

Your Baja mail delivery service will also need to do this. As part of their agreement, they may require you to acknowledge that your packages will be opened. That allows them to clear customs with goods for multiple people and for them to pay the necessary fees. When you hire a service, be sure to inquire about their package policies.

Chapter 12: Baja Life Tips, Customs, and Culture

Day-to-day life in Baja can be whatever you want it to be. Those who prefer solitude will be left alone. Those who want friendship and community will have no trouble finding them. Or any combination thereof. As long as you are a good person who treats others with respect, you will find Mexicans to be extremely accepting people.

Community thrives here in a way that it used to in the United States but rarely does anymore. It's especially essential in the smaller towns and villages, but you'll still find strong communities within the neighborhoods of bigger cities too. In Baja, if anyone needs help, the community immediately rallies, and throughout Baja, neighbors know each other, look out for one another, and help each other.

Soon after I moved there, I began affectionately calling my adopted home of Punta Banda my "Mexican Mayberry." After coming from Los Angeles, it was heartwarming to see how people took care of one another, and especially how they took care of the elderly, both Mexican and expat elderly. Communities here unite for the greater good, and to support the less fortunate.

Those wanting to find friends and activities can be busy every day of the week. There are philanthropic social clubs that support local charities, such as scholarship funds, volunteer fire departments, animal rescues, church groups, and more. Your social calendar will be filled with fun get-togethers, like pickleball, yoga, bridge games, golf and fishing tournaments, food festivals, dining clubs, whale-watching tours, and far too many other activities to list.

After living in Los Angeles for over three decades, small-town life was a refreshing change, most of the time. I say most because the downside is that everyone knows everyone, and gossip can sometimes become an issue. And forget about sneaking out to the corner store or coffee shop in your pajama bottoms to pick up something quickly because you WILL run into someone you know.

Despite any negatives, it's easy to get along here, and a lot of people do – people of all ages, races, religions, sexual orientations, and political philosophies peacefully coexist in Baja. Both the native population and the relocated expats tend to live and let live. Everyone is welcomed as long as that live and let live philosophy is reciprocated and people are treated with respect. If you aren't hurting anybody, the community will accept you, often more than they might in the U.S.

For instance, when I talked to my neighbor Ron Allen, a gay Black man, he said he had no issues being accepted in Baja. An enthusiastic rider and rodeo fan, Ron even told of attending a rural Baja rodeo in high heels and a cowboy hat with zero issues, something he said he could have never done in the States.

Another neighbor, John Kinabrew, has a terrific philosophy for getting along in Baja: "I don't consider myself an expat, I am an immigrant and a guest of this amazing country, and I conduct myself accordingly."

With that philosophy, John and his wife Amy have quickly become treasured and beloved members of their community. It's a good example for all expats to adopt because there is no quicker way to anger the natives than trying to change Baja into the U.S.

Don't Be an Ugly American (or Canadian)!

As accepting as the people of Baja are, there are some expat behaviors that, quite understandably, rile them up. Some of these may be self-evident, others more subtle. In a nutshell, it boils down to, "Don't be a jerk." Act the way you would want all immigrants in the United States to act. Above all else, avoid "Ugly American" behaviors and you will get along fine:

- Don't try to change Mexico into the United States. If you love life in the U.S., you should stay there. Baja is its own place with its own culture, and nothing angers the natives more than Americans moving there only to try to change it into what they left behind. Attempting to import American gun culture is one hot-button example, but there are many others.

- Don't take jobs or business from Mexicans! This rule applies to people working illegally or running businesses under the table. If you are a legal or permanent resident, you do have the right to work or start a business. Otherwise, Mexicans do not like it when immigrants take work from Mexicans any more than Americans do when it happens in the U.S. Sometimes, the offenders do not even realize they are doing anything illegal (not to mention immoral). An example comes to mind of an American expat whose hobby was bread baking. She made amazing breads that she sold to her local expat neighbors. Because it was "just a hobby" and "just to her local village," she saw no harm in this. The problem is there was a local Mexican artisan baker who delivered bread to the village once a week who no longer had enough customers to continue, thanks to this woman's "hobby." Not to mention, if the authorities ever caught on to her illegal business, she would have hefty fines to pay. She might even face deportation, depending on her immigration status. Lastly, these types of illegal off-the-books businesses understandably anger those, both Mexicans and expats, who are doing it the right way and paying their taxes.

- Don't be cheap. I see some people on the expat social media boards (thankfully rarely these days) advising others not to pay much to service people like housekeepers, gardeners, caretakers, and cooks, or they will just "come to expect it." These are often wealthy people, even by U.S. standards, yet they haggle with someone who makes less than $20 a day over two or three dollars. Don't be that jerk! If service people do a good job, pay them well, and you will have loyal help and trustworthy friends throughout your time in Baja. And paying them "well," by Mexican standards will still be a fraction of what it would cost in the U.S. or Canada.

- Tip. This goes hand in hand with the point above, but the 10 to 50 pesos that mean nothing to you can help someone living on poverty wages, like the old man bagging your groceries, tremendously.

- Speak some Spanish. No, you don't have to become fluent, but making some effort at learning a few words, no matter how badly pronounced, can go a long way towards ingratiating yourself to the locals.

- Don't be racist. I am continually shocked by the number of expats who look down on their Mexican neighbors. Usually, it's a passive-aggressive form of racism that the perpetrators themselves sometimes seem oblivious to, and other times it's more overt. Either way and for whatever reasons, if you don't like or respect Mexican people, it's a good idea NOT to move to Mexico.

The Importance of Social Media Groups

For expats in Baja, social media is essential, especially the local Facebook groups. Do a search, and you will find a hierarchy of northern Baja Facebook groups starting in the larger overall region, down to cities and towns, to villages, and in some cases, down to individual neighborhoods and camps. Join the groups for the areas you live in and you will be instantly connected with a community of local people who are willing to help with anything you need or are searching for. You'll also be apprised of local events and happenings ranging from large festivals to charity events to individual birthday gatherings, to daily restaurant specials.

The community Facebook groups are also essential for local news on everything from traffic delays and road closures, to fire and weather emergencies, enhanced police presences, animals on the road, lost dogs and cats, and more. If it is of local importance, people will be discussing it in the Facebook groups.

Of course, like social media groups everywhere, some people fight, and some people are rude internet trolls. Groups with good moderators keep it under control. Nonetheless, people get their panties in a wad and blaze off and start new groups willy-nilly, which can make it confusing for newcomers. My tiny village of Punta Banda has no less than three Facebook groups due to this childish behavior. Ensenada has at least five. Once in an area, you will get a feel for the useful groups as opposed to those started by people who could not get along with others.

One more note about the groups: Take recommendations somewhat with a grain of salt, especially in smaller towns. Everyone knows everyone, and nobody wants to be perceived as a critical jerk, so they only say nice things in public. Likewise, the quality of restaurants and various service businesses is sometimes wildly inflated. Not such a big deal when the end result is a mediocre meal, and the social media boards have steered me to many of those over the years. But they have also steered me to incompetent dentists, veterinarians, computer repair people, and eye doctors. In these cases, I would use the boards for general research, then talk to as many people as possible "off the record."

Feeding Yourself in Baja

Stocking your new home with healthy groceries is easy on the Pacific side of Northern Baja as you have lots of grocery options. Plus, the area south of Ensenada is an enormous agricultural area that supplies a lot of the produce, including organic produce, that's sold in the States.

Things are not as plentiful on the Gulf of California side, but you can still find most grocery items in San Felipe.

- You'll find a variety of supermarket chains on the Pacific side. Soriana, especially Soriana Hipér, stores are giant full-service supermarkets that rival upscale U.S. markets. Calimax is Baja's most prominent grocery store chain and they are comparable to most average American supermarkets. The Mayorista chain caters more to Mexican nationals. While they're not as well stocked with "gringo foods" as the other chains, their prices are generally lower, especially on staples like produce, meat, and dairy.

- If you live in or near Ensenada or Tijuana, you have access to Costco and/or Sam's Club and Wal Mart super stores.

- Supermarkets are not nearly as plentiful on the gulf side of the peninsula, but there is a small Calimax in San Felipe.

- Besides supermarkets, small neighborhood bodega markets, much like the general stores of old, are surprisingly well stocked.

- Local farmer's markets that usually happen once a week sell great produce at shockingly low prices. Sometimes these also include meat and seafood vendors.

- You will find local specialty markets of all kinds, including for seafood, meat, produce, baked goods, cheese, and more.

- Depending on where you live, you may be able to get weekly organic produce boxes for a fraction of what they cost in the States. Usually delivered to one central location at a designated time, your local Facebook group will alert you to this availability.

- Similarly, there may be various food vendors that regularly deliver to the area you live. Fresh seafood, artisan breads, homemade sausages, as well as full homemade meals are offered in my village. Check the local Facebook groups for details.

Dining Out in Baja

There are restaurants at every end of the price and quality spectrum. In the big cities like Tijuana and Ensenada, you will find a wide variety of ethnic restaurants and gourmet cuisine, in addition to U.S. chains and outstanding Mexican fare, of course. In fact, I predict you will no longer want Mexican food in the States after living in Baja (much to the disappointment of friends when you go to visit). Of course, there is a lot of terrific low-cost fare too, especially if you love Mexican food.

Baja is home to some talented and innovative chefs, so discriminating foodies will have fun on lots of fabulous culinary explorations, especially in the Valle de Guadalupe, Tijuana, and Ensenada.

Baja Restaurant Tips

- Sometimes the best food comes from the most humble-looking, hole-in-the-wall stand or street vendor. There are so many of these it's hard to know which are the good ones, but a lot of locals eating there is usually a promising sign.

- Check your checks for accuracy before paying and review your credit card statements after using plastic. Getting overcharged is a common scam, especially in touristy areas. Don't take it personally, it happens to Mexicans as well as gringos.

- Tipping is customary in full-service restaurants. In most instances, tips are pooled and then divided between all the restaurant staff at the end of the night.

- Yelp and Trip Advisor restaurant reviews exist in the bigger cities, but they are not nearly as common as in the U.S.

- Avoid the tamale stands in tourist areas, I have yet to find any that are good. Instead check the Facebook boards and wait until someone's *abuela* (grandmother) is making some for sale.

- Avoiding tourist areas for food, in general, isn't bad advice as you'll be able to find the same or better fare at lower prices elsewhere.

Tacos in Baja

The tacos in Baja (and all of Mexico) are extraordinary, and they are among the cheapest meals to get. But tacos here are not like in the U.S. Each taco stand will have a type of taco they specialize in, so you need to go to the place that serves the kind of tacos you are craving that day. Of course, any and every taco stand worth visiting will serve its tacos on hot, fresh, made-in-front-of-you tortillas.

Taco Stands Fall into 3 Main Categories:

- Seafood: Baja put fish tacos on the map. Besides fish, seafood taco stands will usually also sell shrimp tacos and seafood cocktails, and sometimes seafood *caldo* (soup).

- *Asadero*: Asadero taco stands sell grilled meat tacos, including carne asada beef and achiote-seasoned al pastor pork, and often *cabeza* (head) and *tripa* (tripe) as well. They usually also offer tortas (Mexican sandwiches) and quesadillas too.

- *Birria*: This flavorful slow-cooked bone broth stew is traditionally made with goat but is more frequently found these days with beef. You can buy just the soup, which is laden with meat and veggies, or just the *jugo* (broth), or broth as an accompaniment to tacos made from the slow-cooked meat, either with or without *queso* (cheese).

Side notes:

- You'll rarely see chicken used as a taco ingredient at taco stands in Baja, although there are rotisserie chicken stands everywhere that serve amazing marinated chicken accompanied by tortillas and salsa, so you can make your own. You can find them in sit-down restaurants.

- Burritos are a *gringo* invention. You can find them, but usually not at authentic restaurants. Ditto ground beef, hard-shelled tacos like are served at Taco Bell and other American chain restaurants.

16 Foods and Drinks to Try in Baja

- **Tacos of all kinds:** See above.
- **Seafood Cocktails:** Different than the U.S. versions, these can be shrimp or mixed seafood like shrimp, clams, octopus, and oysters, served in a spicy fresh salsa with avocados and accompanied by saltine crackers.
- **Tortas:** Mexico's national sandwich, tortas come in different varieties, all laden with piles of meat, cheese, and usually avocado, salsa, and veggies, on a hearty roll.
- **Rotisserie Chicken:** Like *El Pollo Loco* in the U.S. but way better.
- **Carnitas:** A dish made by braising pork in its own fat, like rotisserie chicken, carnitas are sold accompanied by tortillas and salsa. Some of the best carnitas places seem to be little mom-and-pop shops that are only open on the weekends.
- **Chicharrónes:** Get these crispy fried pork rinds freshly made at the same places that sell carnitas.
- **Street Corn:** Mexico's favorite street food, fresh corn (*elote*), on the cob or in a glass (*en vaso*), with butter, mayonnaise, spices, and cheese, has now taken the world by storm, but it's readily available everywhere in Baja.
- **Chilaquiles:** A dish of fresh tortilla chips coated in a red or green salsa may not sound exciting, but chilaquiles are awesome, with or without toppings.
- **Paletas:** These delicious frozen treats on a stick made from fresh fruits and sometimes dairy products, in a huge array of flavors, are especially popular in summer.

- **Margaritas:** Unless it is a cheesy restaurant in a tourist zone, these will always be made completely from scratch in Baja. No powdered sweet and sour premix here. That's usually the same case with all cocktails. While in the U.S. they would be labeled "artisan" and hit with a higher price tag, in Baja it's just the way they make drinks.

- **Micheladas:** This beer-based version of a hot sauce-enhanced Bloody Mary (no vodka) served in a chilled salt-rimmed glass makes a lighter alcohol brunch option.

- **Aguas Frescas:** Available in a variety of flavors, these are light, refreshing, nonalcoholic drinks, served from large jars and made from fresh fruits and sometimes flowers, rice, nuts, and/or milk.

- **Tres Leches Cake:** The national cake of Mexico, you'll find lots of varieties on the basic theme at every Mexican bakery.

- **Juices and Smoothies:** Fresh squeezed juice and smoothie stands are abundant in Baja.

- **Fruit Bowls:** Amazing fresh fruit bowls are offered by street vendors all over Baja, but they're my favorite thing to get while waiting in line to cross the border.

- **Tepache:** This healthy, probiotic, fermented pineapple drink is sold all over by street vendors, but I also like to make my own at home.

- **Churros:** The popular, fried cinnamon and sugar-covered lengths of fried dough can be sublime if you get them hot out of the fryer. Otherwise, they are not worth the calories, and cold churros can be gross and greasy. Always insist on "*churros calientes*" from the vendor.

Border Crossing Tips and Strategies

Unless you are a permanent resident who never wants to leave Baja, and I do know a lot of such folks, border crossings are a fact of life for Baja expats. In the best of circumstances, it's just a short delay in your travel plans, and you are on your way. In the worst of circumstances, it can mean hours of waiting in line in your vehicle and intense border inspections.

There are things you can do to help avoid border crossing stress; however, sometimes, there is simply no way to know in advance what you will encounter. I call it the border crapshoot. You'll almost never know the exact cause of the delays, but border crossings can back up for six hours or more, for instance, if the police are looking for fugitives or have tips about contraband shipments.

A lot of west coast Baja expats I know prefer to cross at the smaller border crossings like Otay Mesa or Tecate, as opposed to the world's busiest land border crossing in San Ysidro. I have found this to only be somewhat successful. While the smaller crossings service far less daily traffic, they also have far fewer lanes, and they can likewise backlog quickly if there are any incidents out of the ordinary. This is not to say that San Ysidro doesn't back up, too; it does every day without fail. But under normal circumstances, it moves fairly quickly. The smaller crossings, unlike San Ysidro, are not open 24 hours a day either.

Border Crossing Tips When Going into the United States

Anytime I can cross the border going into the United States in an hour or less, I consider it a victory. It can be done, even if you do not have a SENTRI card.. These tips can help:

- If you qualify, get a SENTRI card from the U.S. State Department. This advanced security clearance allows you to access special express border crossing lines (it has other international travel benefits at airports too). Everyone in the vehicle, not just the driver, must have a SENTRI card to use the special lanes. Get more information on how to apply here: cbp.gov

- When possible, avoid crossing on Sunday afternoons and early evenings or any days when American tourists are returning home after a holiday.

- Time crossing to avoid rush hours. Usually, between 10 in the morning until about 1 in the afternoon is not bad, and again at 7 to 9 in the evenings.

- Never trust the online and radio border crossing wait times as they are typically inaccurate by an hour or more.

Border Crossing When Going Into Mexico

Crossing into Mexico is usually far easier and less time-consuming than going the other way, although in San Ysidro, the U.S. has sometimes started screening people who leave the country, which is causing delays before you even get to the Mexican border that never existed before. This border crossing can also back up during San Diego's rush hour traffic in the mornings and evenings.

In most instances, unless you have goods worth over $300 to declare, you won't even be stopped when going into Mexico. It is always possible though, as cars are randomly flagged for inspection by Mexican border control agents. No need to panic if this happens unless you are carrying contraband. Or if you have goods in excess of $300 in value or that look like stock for sale, in which case you will have to go inside and pay a fine.

If it is your first time in Baja you will also need to stop to validate your FMM card (see Chapter 5).

Tips on Tipping

Baja runs on tips or *propinas*. A minuscule amount of money to us, placed in the right hands, can make big differences in the lives of people struggling to survive. It can also vastly improve your levels of comfort and service.

Unlike in the U.S., panhandling is rare. Mexicans are hardworking and proud people, so even when asking strangers for money, there is usually some kind of goods or services exchanged. There are exceptions at the borders, but these people are typically severely disabled.

I love some of the services I get by tipping. For instance, getting the car windows washed, or people waiting outside of Costco in Ensenada who will happily take your cart, follow you to your car, and unload all your heavy groceries. Well worth a tip!

A common sight in supermarkets is elderly men and women who bag the groceries. With few exceptions, these are not paid store employees but rather workers who survive only on tips (there is no senior social safety net in Mexico). Generously tip one of these folks and I guarantee you'll see a big smile. They won't forget you next time either as you have a friend for life. There have even been days when I am out of change and my favorite baggers know I am good for it next time.

While the people pumping your gas at fuel stations are getting paid, I know they don't get paid much, so I usually tip them too, especially when they wash the windows or check the oil, which they will if you ask. The same with the guys delivering water or propane. When in doubt, offer a tip.

Tipping in full-service restaurants is expected. Most of the time, the tips are split between all of the restaurant staff at the end of the night.

Speaking of tipping, be sure to see below about Christmas bonuses because Mexicans take Christmas bonuses extremely seriously!

Christmas Bonuses – Not Just a Good Idea, It's the Law

Mexico takes Christmas bonuses seriously! The aguinaldo is a yearly holiday bonus that employers in Mexico are legally required to give to their employees by December 20th. The minimum required amount is 15 days' worth of the employee's daily wages for those who have completed a full year of service, although many employers provide more as a goodwill gesture. Those who have not completed a full year of service are entitled to receive a proportionate

---

share of the bonus, depending on the number of weeks or months the employee has worked.

You may think as a non-business owner in Baja that paying an *aguinaldo* does not apply to you, but you would probably be wrong. If you regularly employ domestic workers like housekeepers, gardeners, or nannies, you should pay them an *aguinaldo*. Also, if you live in a camp or planned neighborhood, it is customary for each of the residents to give each of the workers in the camp, like the security guards, gardeners, and maintenance people, a small holiday bonus of about 100 pesos, tucked into a Christmas card. The more the employee helps you or the more you interact with them, the more you should give them. The landlord will often assist by distributing a list of qualified employees to camp residents in early December. While you are not legally obligated to do this, it would be extremely bad form not to.

More than just an extra bonus, many Mexican workers depend on the *aguinaldo* to get them and their families through the holidays and beyond. The practice also boosts local economies during the holidays as workers spend the money.

Cultural Differences You Need to Know

I could write an entire book about the cultural differences between the United States and Baja, so this will only touch on a few points that might directly affect your Baja experience in the short term. Of course, some of the points are generalities, but they do represent the cultural norms in Baja.

- The biggest issues come when foreigners try to schedule things or do things. Mexicans tend to have a cultural aversion to saying no directly, so instead of refusing a job or invitation, they are apt to be more noncommittal, which can leave you wondering what happened when someone doesn't show up, or why you can't get an answer. If someone is not returning your calls or being vague, chances are the answer is no, they just don't know how to politely tell you that.

- Your best chance of getting answers and scheduling is by using WhatsApp (see Chapter 11).

- Mexicans are almost NEVER in a hurry. The hectic, rushed culture of the U.S. does not exist in Baja, which is known for its laid-back lifestyle. Things start and end when they do. Even socially, it's not uncommon for people to arrive at parties hours late.

- Know that *mañana* does not necessarily mean tomorrow, it just means not today. A better question to ask when trying to schedule something would be *cuál dia* (which day).

- Generally speaking, Mexicans go out of their way to always be polite and accommodating. Being rude and demanding, or expressing your anger to strangers, no matter how frustrated you are, will not help your cause. Don't be a "Karen."

Conclusion

I hope you found this book useful in your explorations of a move to Baja California, Mexico. I tried to include every decision and obstacle I encountered when moving to Baja, along with the questions I am commonly asked. I also tried to include as much practical information about the move itself too, so that the process would be easier for my readers than it was when I had to piecemeal research together.

This brings me to my next point: Get ready for lots of people to ask you about your experiences if you decide to relocate to Baja. Many people are looking for a better, more affordable, and more sustainable lifestyle, and making a move like this will always be a conversation starter, no matter where you are in the world.

Before we sign off, if you got value out of this book, please do me a HUGE favor and post an honest review on Amazon. It takes just a few seconds and costs nothing, but it will help this information be found by more people who need it.

Thank you so much and I hope to see you in Baja! (*Muchas gracias y espero verte en Baja!*)

Resources:

- Find the official Mexican government website at gob.mx.
- Apply for your FMM (tourist visa) card online. inm.gob.mx/fmme/publico/en/solicitud
- Temporary Residency for Americans. consulmex.sre.gob.mx
- Temporary Residency for Canadians. consulmex.sre.gob.mx
- Permanent Residency for Americans. consulmex.sre.gob.mx
- Permanent Residency for Canadians consulmex.sre.gob.mx

News: *Mexico News Daily* is an excellent source for Mexican news and culture, in English. mexiconewsdaily.com

Language: Baselang is the best deal I have found on language tutors and one of the best ways to get fluent in Spanish. For a reasonable monthly price, you get UNLIMITED one-on-one online Spanish tutoring classes. baselang.com

Attorney: Locate Carlos Victorica Reyes, who consulted on this book, at expatguardian.com.

Acknowledgments

This book would not have been possible without the help, support, and input of so many people that I need to thank, especially my amazing Mexican attorney, Carlos Victorica Reyes, who provided invaluable insight and consultation on topics like immigration, residency, property ownership, business ownership, and more. Because he understands the laws and culture on both sides of the border so well, Carlos has a way of making everything accessible and understandable and I am immensely grateful for his guidance in tackling these complicated subjects.

Thank you also to my Baja friends who shared their experiences and insights, especially Sitara Monica Perez, Thomas Rogan, Renata Rogan, Ron Allen, John Kinabrew, Amy DeBaun, Kristina Gandy, David Gandy, and Gabriela Victorica McEntee.

Thank you to Vanessa Waltz, Darlene Williams Bostock, and Tracy Burnes for their help in finalizing the manuscript, and to my editor Maybelle Drakis for all her hard work whipping it into shape.

And last, but certainly not least, thank you to my incredible family, Richard Burnes and Tracy Burnes, for giving me an amazing space to write this book, and for your perpetual love and support.

About the Author

Cheri Sicard is the author of nine published books on topics as diverse as US Citizenship to Cannabis Cooking. In 2017, after decades of living in Los Angeles, she and her business partner moved to Baja California, Mexico, where they fulfilled a lifelong dream to live on a beach. This book is the culmination of years of answering questions from friends and acquaintances about how they can live a more vibrant and affordable life in Mexico too.

www.ingramcontent.com/pod-product-compliance
Lightning Source LLC
Chambersburg PA
CBHW071225090426
42736CB00014B/2980